How to use this book

The Flowers are arranged by family, following the normal sequence. All the most common and striking British flowers are included. In addition, there are illustrations and descriptions of the grasses, sedges, rushes and ferns most likely to be encountered in the countryside.

The Introduction. This provides, clearly and simply, a brief introduction to the study and recognition of wild flowers. All the terms used throughout the main text are explained and there are descriptions of different habitats that wild flowers occupy in Britain.

There is an illustrated key to the contents of the book. Representative members of the different families are illustrated as an aid to rapid identification.

Hints on identification. Always use both text and illustration together. Neither is complete without the other. The text stresses those aspects of the appearance of the flower which distinguish it from other similar flowers.

In time it becomes easy to recognise the groups to which most flowers belong and you will be able to turn to the relevant section of the book without trouble. To begin with, it is probably best to concentrate on a few key features. These include the number of petals, whether the flowers grow singly or in clusters, and colour of the flower. Also important are the general habit of growth – whether the plant is creeping or upright for example – and the sort of habitat in which it is found.

Conservation. Our wild flowers are both precious and vulnerable. Flowers that are picked cannot set seed to provide for a new generation. Always remember therefore to take the book to the plant and not the plant to the book. There is as much pleasure to be had from sketching or photographing wild flowers as there is from pressing them or having them for a few hours in a vase.

A HANDGUIDE TO THE
WILD
FLOWERS
OF BRITAIN AND NORTHERN EUROPE

Painted by **Marjorie Blamey**

Text by **Richard Fitter**

TREASURE PRESS

ACKNOWLEDGEMENTS

This title first appeared as the *Collins Handguide to the Wild Flowers of Britain and Europe* and Treasure Press gratefully acknowledge the co-operation of William Collins Sons & Co Ltd who gave permission for this edition to be published.

First published in Great Britain in 1979 by
William Collins Sons & Co Ltd

This edition published in 1985 by
Treasure Press
Michelin House
81 Fulham Road
London SW3 6RB

Reprinted 1988, 1989, 1990

ISBN 1 85051 051 2

Printed in Portugal by Oficinas Gráficas ASA

Contents

Illustrations show representative flowers of the commoner groups as an aid to initial identification.

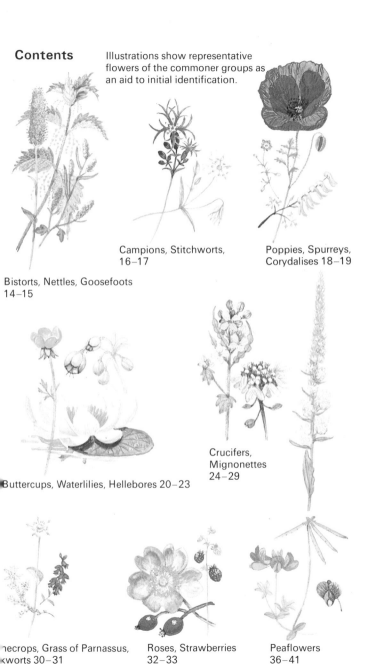

3

Wood Sorrel, Cranesbills
42–43

Mallows, Flaxes
44–45

St John's Worts, Violets,
Rock-rose 46–47

Willowherbs,
Evening Primrose
48–49

Umbellifers, Daphnes,
White Bryony, Ivy
50–51

White Umbellifers,
Wintergreens 52–55

Heaths
Crowberr
56–57

Primroses, Pimpernels
58–59

Periwinkles, Gentians,
60–61

Bedstraws, Cleavers
62–63

Bindweeds, Nightshades
64–65

Forgetmenots, Buglosses
66–67

Labiates 68–73

Speedwells, Louseworts
74–77

Foxglove, Butterworts,
Plantains 78–79

Honeysuckles, Valerians,
Teasels 80–81

Scabiouses, Bellflowers,
Lobelias 81, 82–83

Composites 84–97

Arrowhead, 98–99

Fritillary, Grape Hyacinth
100–102

Daffodil, Iris, Black Bryony
102–103

Orchids
104–111

Grasses 116–121

Rushes, Sedges
112–115

Ferns 122–123

5

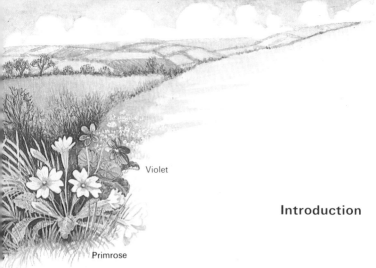

Violet

Primrose

Introduction

The great majority of the wild flowers you are likely to see in walks about the countryside are illustrated here. Most of the exceptions are so similar to the wild flowers described here that the ordinary country lover would not be likely to notice the difference. Trees and shrubs with inconspicuous flowers, which are also flowering plants, are omitted. Trees are the subject of a separate Handguide by John Wilkinson and Alan Mitchell. A small number of rushes, sedges and grasses are also included, as well as a few ferns and horsetails, which reproduce themselves by spores instead of seeds and so are not flowering plants.

Almost all the wild flowers in the book grow wild in the British Isles: Great Britain, Ireland, the Isle of Man and the Channel Islands, with their various offshore islands, such as the Scilly Isles, Orkney and Shetland. Some are more widely found on the Continent. All the plants in the book grow north of the Loire and the Alps and east approximately to the eastern borders of West Germany and Sweden, so that it covers the whole of Belgium, Denmark, Luxemburg and the Netherlands, the greater part of Norway, Sweden and West Germany, and the northern half of France. Beyond these limits the flora of the Mediterranean, the Alps, the steppes and the Arctic begins to show great differences from that of Britain and northwestern Europe.

Technical terms have been kept to a minimum, but a few must be learned if the description of a wild flower is to make any sense. Most important of these are petal, sepal, stamen, anther, style and stigma. Flowers are the reproductive parts of plants, and the most important reproductive organs have both to be protected against the elements and made conspicuous enough to attract the pollinators to them. The protective function is performed by the *sepals*, the ring of outer parts of the flower, usually green. The *petals*, the inner ring, usually brightly coloured, serve both to protect, when they are folded inwards – some flowers such as scarlet pimpernel,

| Petal | Sepals | Stamens and anthers | Stigma and styles |

fold inwards whenever the sun goes in – and to attract pollinating insects to the flowers. Either petals or sepals may be missing; and in some plants, such as the Marsh Marigold, the sepals may be brightly coloured like petals. A few plants, notably the spurges (p 44), have neither petals nor sepals, but these species often have other cup-like structures that mimic the sepals. Plants of the Daisy Family, as indicated on p 84, have all these features, but their small flowers are gathered together in a head that resembles a single large flower.

In the centre of the flower lie the male and female reproductive organs. The male ones, called *stamens*, end in an *anther*, on which the pollen develops. The female, called *styles*, end in a *stigma*, to which the pollen is transferred, and below these are the ovaries, which, when fertilised, develop into the fruits or seeds. Pollination is achieved either by the wind, in which case the actual flower does not need to be very conspicuous, or by an insect or other invertebrate, which must be attracted to the flower in order to do the job, in the hope of reward. Nectar is the reward of the pollinator, which is attracted either by scent, or by colour. Night-flying insects, especially moths, are attracted by white flowers, which show up better in the dusk; yellow, blue, purple or red flowers are designed to lure day fliers, such as bees and butterflies.

The seeds, once formed, may be dispersed in a number of different ways. The heavier ones just drop to the ground. Lighter ones blow away in the wind, and this process may be aided by special devices, such as the pappuses which form on fruiting dandelions and make the dandelion 'clock'. Yet other fruits have to pass through the gut of a mammal or bird, whose digestive juices play an important part in softening the hard seed-coat to enable the seed to germinate.

Scarlet Pimpernel

7

Ecology and Habitat

Anybody who walks about the countryside soon realises that he or she sees different plants in different types of habitat. You do not expect to find a primrose on the seashore, or a foxglove growing among the waterlilies. Three main factors determine where plants grow: warmth and cold, which depend on the climate; dryness and wetness, which depend on a combination of the climate and the soil; and the nutrient minerals in the soil. Apart from local variations, such as the shelter provided by rocks, trees, and deep valleys, it gets colder as you go north, uphill and away from the warming influence of the Gulf Stream; and it gets wetter as you go west and uphill. The result is that Britain is divided into roughly four quadrants: the south-east is dry and warm, the south-west wet and warm, the north-west wet and cold and the north-east dry and cold. The big divide in soil conditions is between the alkaline soils of chalk and limestone, and the acid soils of the sands, gravels and gritstones. The coast brings a further complication, because some plants can stand salt in the soil and others cannot.

Groundsel

Shepherd's Purse

Red Dead-nettle

The main habitat groups of plants are those of bare ground, grassland, woodland, heath and moor, fresh water and the coast.

Plants of Bare Ground and Grassland

The plants of bare ground include many of the common garden weeds, such as Groundsel, Shepherd's Purse, Common Field Speedwell, Red Dead-nettle and Petty Spurge. A more specialised group of bare-ground plants are those that grow on walls, such as Wallflower, Ivy-leaved Bell-flower and various stonecrops. Such annual plants, known as pioneers, cannot stand much competition from other plants. Therefore, as soon as

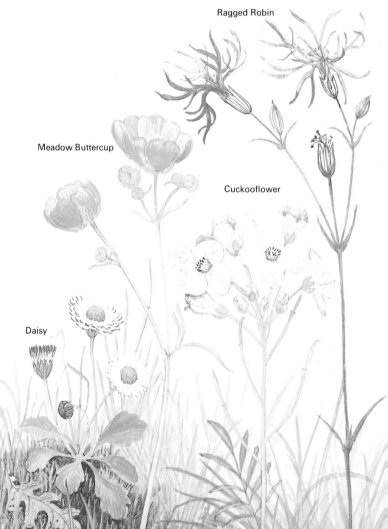

Ragged Robin

Meadow Buttercup

Cuckooflower

Daisy

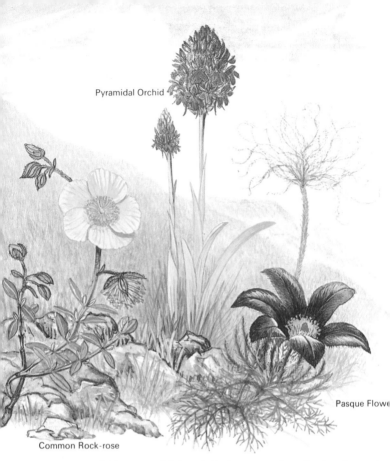

Pyramidal Orchid

Pasque Flower

Common Rock-rose

grasses and other perennials invade the bare ground – and nature does not leave any piece of ground bare for long, unless it is devoid of nutrients altogether – they give way to the plants of grassland, such as buttercups, Daisy, Common Sorrel, Common Mouse-ear and Black Knapweed. In damper grassland you will find such delectable species as Lady's Smock, Ragged Robin, Marsh Orchids, Marsh Marigold and Meadow Thistle. On the chalk downs there is again a great array of attractive lime-loving wild flowers, such as Pasque Flower, Common Rockrose, Common and Chalk Milkworts and Pyramidal, Fragrant and Common Spotted Orchids, that are found nowhere else.

Grassland is only prevented from developing into first scrub and later woodland by some interference from man or animals, such as grazing by deer, sheep or cattle, mowing, or trampling. Genuine sheep-cropped downland turf is now becoming very scarce. Much downland has been ploughed up and in some areas most of the surviving downland flowers are to be found on the road verges.

Plants of Woodland

Woodland too has many plants that do not grow elsewhere, such as Wood Anemone, Wood Sorrel, Woodruff, Wood Forgetmenot and Dog's Mercury. As with grassland, so the woods that lie on chalk and limestone have their own specialities, such as Green and Stinking Hellebores, Birdsnest and Large White Helleborine Orchids, Mezereon, Spurge Laurel and Lily of the Valley. Some plants, such as Primrose and Bluebell, are able to grow in woods because there are no leaves on the trees in early spring, when they first bloom. They are thus able to get the light they need. Such plants may also be found in open situations, such as railway banks and sea cliffs, where they also get plenty of light before bracken, tall grasses and other plants grow up in the summer.

Only in Scotland are native coniferous woods to be found, but these have a special flora of their own, which includes several wintergreens, Creeping Lady's Tresses Orchid and the delicate little Twinflower, the favourite of the great Swedish botanist Linnaeus. Indeed so fond of it was he that he named it *Linnaea borealis* after himself. The tree that forms these native coniferous woodlands is the Scots Pine. The only other trees that form extensive woodlands in Britain are oak, of which there are two species, the Pedunculate Oak and the Durmast Oak, Beech and Ash. Beech and Ash form woods mainly on limestone or chalk. In a few areas birchwoods also occur, and there are still a diminishing number of alder woods, or alder carrs, in damp valley bottoms.

Bluebell

Wood Sorrel

Bracken

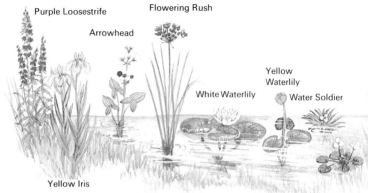

Purple Loosestrife
Flowering Rush
Arrowhead
Yellow Waterlily
White Waterlily
Water Soldier
Yellow Iris
Frogbit

Plants of Water and the Waterside

Fresh water too has a whole array of plants that do not grow anywhere else. Some of these, such as Purple and Yellow Loosestrifes, Yellow Flag, Great Willowherb, Marsh Woundwort and Water Figwort, grow on the banks. Others, such as Flowering Rush, Arrowhead, Common Club-rush and Common Reed, have their feet well in the water. Yet others, such as the White and Yellow Water-lilies, are rooted in the bottom but have their flowers on the surface, while there are even one or two, such as the Frogbit and the Water Soldier, and of course the ubiquitous duckweeds, that just float.

By the sea each sub-habitat also has its special plants. Sea Rocket and Saltwort grow on the strand-line, Yellow Horned Poppy, Sea Sandwort and Sea Holly and Sea Bindweed on the shingle, and Sea Spurreys, Sea-lavenders and Sea Purslane on the saltmarsh. Sand dunes form a curious link between the shore and the chalk downs, for they usually have limy soil and so many of the chalk-loving plants also grow there.

Yellow Horned Poppy

Heather

Bog Asphodel

Plants of Heath and Moor

Heaths are the lowland and moors the upland vegetation that overlie mainly acid soils, but like grassland they are prevented from becoming woods by some such factor as grazing or fire. They have many special plants, the shrubs Gorse and Broom, the undershrubs Heather and Bell Heather, and such attractive wild flowers as Tormentil, Heath Milkwort, and in wetter places the Yellow Iris.

All these wild flowers are under increasing threat from the spread of modern civilisation. Agriculture, industry, forestry, housing development, all encroach on the rapidly diminishing semi-natural habitats where most of the more interesting and attractive wild flowers grow. Only the weeds of bare ground thrive and spread. What you can do to help preserve our wild flora is quite simple. Never dig up a wild plant, Pick only sparingly of the commonest species. Take care where you trample if you go off the footpath. And join your county naturalists' trust, which is establishing local reserves to save the most threatened flora. You can get its address from the Society for the Promotion of Nature Conservation, The Green, Nettleham, Lincoln.

DOCKS, SORRELS, NETTLES & GOOSEFOOTS

The Bistort Family (Polygonaceae) has two distinctive groups of plants –
the bistorts proper and the docks and sorrels. Bistorts have papery whitish
sheaths at the base of their leaves and small five-petalled flowers.
Bistort *Polygonum bistorta* (1) grows in patches in meadows and open
woods, often near water.

Redshank or **Persicaria**
P. persicaria (2) is a common
weed with straggly reddish stems:
its leaves often have a dark spot,
its flowers may be pink or white.
Knotgrass *P. aviculare* (3) is
another very common weed, also
growing on sea-shores, whose
flowers may be either pink or
white.

The docks and sorrels have six-petalled green flowers that are often strongly tinged red. **Broad-leaved Dock** *Rumex obtusifolius* (4) is an abundant weed with leaves up to 30 cm long. **Water Dock** *R. hydrolapathum* (5) grows to 2 m tall, with leaves up to 1 m long, by rivers and ponds. **Common Sorrel** *R. acetosa* (6) is the plant that tinges the meadows red in May and June. Its leaves taste slightly acid.

The Nettle Family (Urticaceae) has tiny greenish flowers in catkins, with yellow stamens. **Stinging Nettle** *Urtica dioica* (10), with powerful stinging hairs, is a food plant for butterflies. **Pellitory of the Wall** *Parietaria judaica* (9) grows on rocks, banks and walls, and does not sting. The Goosefoot Family (Chenopodiaceae), with tiny green petal-less flowers, grow as weeds on bare ground. **Fat Hen** *Chenopodium album* (7), a prehistoric and mediaeval food plant, has leaves covered with whitish meal. (The late-flowering Red Goosefoot *C. rubrum* has green leaves and often grows on manure heaps.)

Common Orache *Atriplex patula* (8) is a weed of cultivation which often grows on sea-shores. It has narrow leaves, the basal lobes pointing forwards.

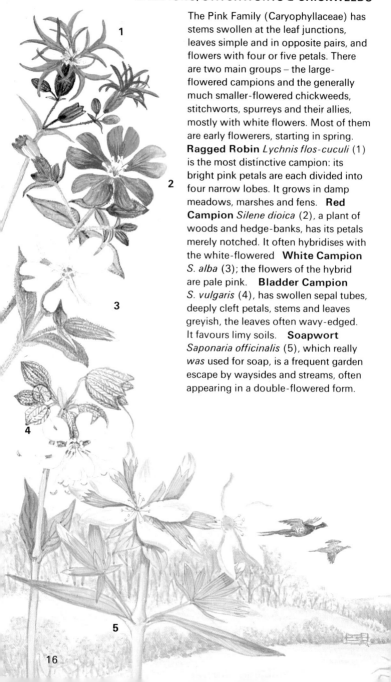

CAMPIONS, STITCHWORTS & CHICKWEEDS

The Pink Family (Caryophyllaceae) has stems swollen at the leaf junctions, leaves simple and in opposite pairs, and flowers with four or five petals. There are two main groups – the large-flowered campions and the generally much smaller-flowered chickweeds, stitchworts, spurreys and their allies, mostly with white flowers. Most of them are early flowerers, starting in spring. **Ragged Robin** *Lychnis flos-cuculi* (1) is the most distinctive campion: its bright pink petals are each divided into four narrow lobes. It grows in damp meadows, marshes and fens. **Red Campion** *Silene dioica* (2), a plant of woods and hedge-banks, has its petals merely notched. It often hybridises with the white-flowered **White Campion** *S. alba* (3); the flowers of the hybrid are pale pink. **Bladder Campion** *S. vulgaris* (4), has swollen sepal tubes, deeply cleft petals, stems and leaves greyish, the leaves often wavy-edged. It favours limy soils. **Soapwort** *Saponaria officinalis* (5), which really *was* used for soap, is a frequent garden escape by waysides and streams, often appearing in a double-flowered form.

Thyme-leaved Sandwort *Arenaria serpyllifolia* (6) has unnotched petals and grows on walls and other dry bare places.

Mouse-ears *Cerastium* have their petals notched. **Common-Mouse-ear** *C. fontanum* (7) is a very common plant of grassy and waste places. Sticky Mouse-ear *C. glomeratum*, stickily hairy and with its flowers in tight heads and often scarcely opening, grows on bare ground only. The largest-flowered is **Field Mouse-ear** *C. arvense* (8) with downy leaves, growing in dry open grassland on limy soils. It must not be confused with the common garden escape Dusty Miller *C. tomentosum* whose stems and leaves are thickly covered with white hairs. Stitchworts *Stellaria* have their white petals deeply cleft, often to the base. **Greater Stitchwort** *S. holostea* (10) has the largest flowers, and square stems, and grows mainly in hedge-banks in the spring. **Lesser Stitchwort** *S. graminea* is a later-flowering miniature version of grassy and heathy places that avoids limy soils. A broader-leaved plant with flowers between these two in size growing by fresh water and not flowering till summer is likely to be Water Chickweed *Myosoton aquaticum*. **Common Chickweed** *S. media* (9) is one of the commonest weeds of cultivated ground and flowers all the year round. A taller plant that flowers in woodlands in spring and has prominently veined leaves is Three-veined Sandwort *Moehringia trinervia*.

10

8

9

7

6

Sea Sandwort *Honkenya peploides* (1) is a creeping plant of sand and shingle by the sea, with fleshy yellow-green leaves. Sea Spurreys *Spergularia* are pink-flowered chickweed-like plants, with a whitish scale at the base of their narrow fleshy leaves. **Greater Sea Spurrey** *S. media* (2) has its petals longer than its sepals, and Lesser Sea Spurrey *S. marina* has them shorter; both grow in saltmarshes. Rock Sea Spurrey *S. rupicola*, with petals equalling sepals, grows on sea-cliffs and rocks. The stickily hairy Sand Spurrey *S. rubra* grows in sandy places inland. **Corn Spurrey** *Spergula arvensis* (3), a frequent weed, looks quite different with its white flowers and whorls of longer leaves.

The Poppy Family (Papaveraceae) is divided into two distinct groups: the poppies and celandine with four petals and milky juice in their stems; and the fumitories and corydalises with spikes of spurred tabular flowers and leaves more elaborately divided.

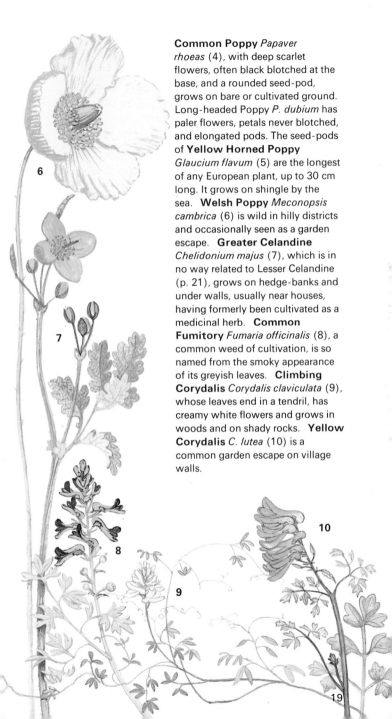

Common Poppy *Papaver rhoeas* (4), with deep scarlet flowers, often black blotched at the base, and a rounded seed-pod, grows on bare or cultivated ground. Long-headed Poppy *P. dubium* has paler flowers, petals never blotched, and elongated pods. The seed-pods of **Yellow Horned Poppy** *Glaucium flavum* (5) are the longest of any European plant, up to 30 cm long. It grows on shingle by the sea. **Welsh Poppy** *Meconopsis cambrica* (6) is wild in hilly districts and occasionally seen as a garden escape. **Greater Celandine** *Chelidonium majus* (7), which is in no way related to Lesser Celandine (p. 21), grows on hedge-banks and under walls, usually near houses, having formerly been cultivated as a medicinal herb. **Common Fumitory** *Fumaria officinalis* (8), a common weed of cultivation, is so named from the smoky appearance of its greyish leaves. **Climbing Corydalis** *Corydalis claviculata* (9), whose leaves end in a tendril, has creamy white flowers and grows in woods and on shady rocks. **Yellow Corydalis** *C. lutea* (10) is a common garden escape on village walls.

BUTTERCUPS, SPEARWORTS & MEADOW-RUES

The Buttercup Family (Ranunculaceae) are very varied in appearance and by no means all members resemble the buttercups proper, *Ranunculus*, with their shiny bright yellow five-petalled flowers. Three species of buttercup grow commonly in grassy places: the tall **Meadow Buttercup** *R. acris* (1), with the end lobe of each leaf stalked; the shorter **Bulbous Buttercup** *R. bulbosus* (2), best recognised by its down-turned sepals, which likes limy soils; and the **Creeping Buttercup** *R. repens* (3), which has rooting runners and grows in damper, often bare places. The first two are the flowers that make our meadows yellow in May and June. **Goldilocks Buttercup** *R. auricomus* (4) grows in woods and on shady banks, and often has ragged petals or even none at all.

Lesser Spearwort *R. flammula* (5), with
narrow leaves, grows in marshes and wet
places. Greater Spearwort *R. lingua*, much
taller and with flowers 25 mm across, is less
common. **Celery-leaved Buttercup**
R. sceleratus (6), another mud-lover, has
smaller flowers and shiny leaves.
Lesser Celandine *R. ficaria* (7), a common
early spring flower of woods, hedge-banks and
damp bare ground, has from eight to a dozen
narrower petals. It is no relation of Greater
Celandine (p. 19). **Marsh Marigold** *Caltha
palustris* (8), is an early-flowering outsize
buttercup of wet places, with flowers
25–50 mm across. The equally wide globular
yellow flowers of **Globe Flower** *Trollius
europaeus* (10), are unmistakable. It grows in
grassy places in the hills. The flowers of
Meadow-rues, *Thalictrum*, are conspicuous
mainly for their fuzz of yellow stamens.
Common Meadow-rue *T. flavum* (9) is a
tall plant of damp meadows and watersides.
Lesser Meadow-rue, *T. minus*, is usually
shorter and grows on limestone rocks and
grassland, sand dunes by the sea, and river
shingle.

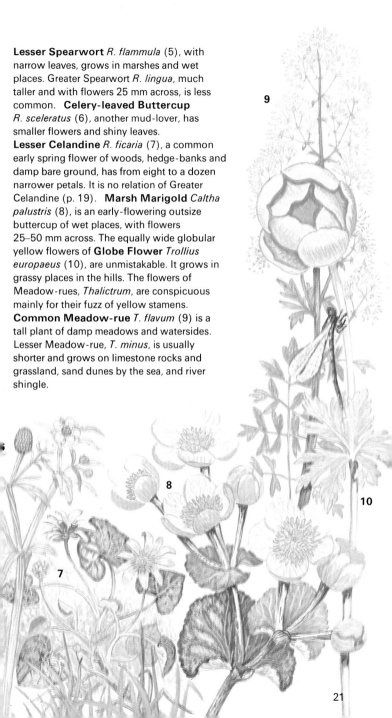

The **Wood Anemone** *Anemone nemorosa* (1), a member of the Buttercup Family, carpets the woodlands in spring. It has white petal-like sepals often tinged pink on the back. The magnificent **Pasque Flower** *Pulsatilla vulgaris* (2) is so named because it flowers at Easter, which is *Pâques* in French. The long silky plumes of the fruits persist well into the summer. **Columbine** *Aquilegia vulgaris* (3) is much less common as a wild than as a garden plant. It grows in woods and scrub on limy soils. Our two hellebores (*Helleborus*) both grow in woods on limy soils, and flower in late winter and early spring. **Stinking Hellebore** *H. foetidus* (4) is a tall, almost bushy plant, with bell-shaped flowers and yellow-green petal-like sepals tipped with purple. **Green Hellebore** *H. viridis* (5) is low growing with larger, more open flowers, and leaves that do not appear till the flowers are open.

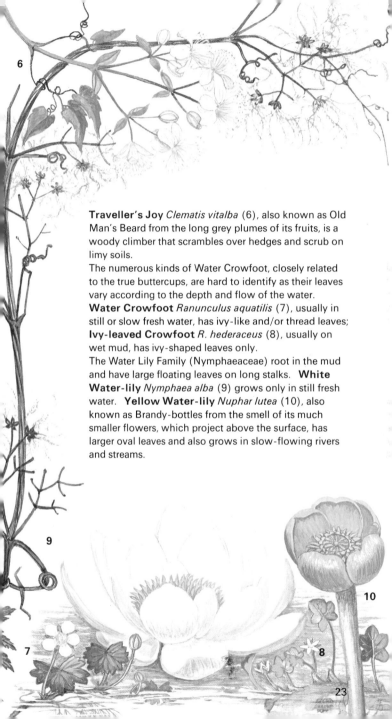

Traveller's Joy *Clematis vitalba* (6), also known as Old Man's Beard from the long grey plumes of its fruits, is a woody climber that scrambles over hedges and scrub on limy soils.

The numerous kinds of Water Crowfoot, closely related to the true buttercups, are hard to identify as their leaves vary according to the depth and flow of the water.

Water Crowfoot *Ranunculus aquatilis* (7), usually in still or slow fresh water, has ivy-like and/or thread leaves; **Ivy-leaved Crowfoot** *R. hederaceus* (8), usually on wet mud, has ivy-shaped leaves only.

The Water Lily Family (Nymphaeaceae) root in the mud and have large floating leaves on long stalks. **White Water-lily** *Nymphaea alba* (9) grows only in still fresh water. **Yellow Water-lily** *Nuphar lutea* (10), also known as Brandy-bottles from the smell of its much smaller flowers, which project above the surface, has larger oval leaves and also grows in slow-flowing rivers and streams.

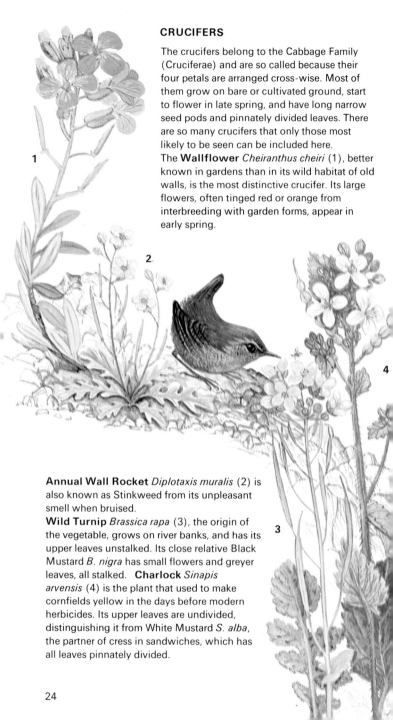

CRUCIFERS

The crucifers belong to the Cabbage Family
(Cruciferae) and are so called because their
four petals are arranged cross-wise. Most of
them grow on bare or cultivated ground, start
to flower in late spring, and have long narrow
seed pods and pinnately divided leaves. There
are so many crucifers that only those most
likely to be seen can be included here.

The **Wallflower** *Cheiranthus cheiri* (1), better
known in gardens than in its wild habitat of old
walls, is the most distinctive crucifer. Its
large flowers, often tinged red or orange from
interbreeding with garden forms, appear in
early spring.

Annual Wall Rocket *Diplotaxis muralis* (2) is
also known as Stinkweed from its unpleasant
smell when bruised.

Wild Turnip *Brassica rapa* (3), the origin of
the vegetable, grows on river banks, and has its
upper leaves unstalked. Its close relative Black
Mustard *B. nigra* has small flowers and greyer
leaves, all stalked. **Charlock** *Sinapis
arvensis* (4) is the plant that used to make
cornfields yellow in the days before modern
herbicides. Its upper leaves are undivided,
distinguishing it from White Mustard *S. alba*,
the partner of cress in sandwiches, which has
all leaves pinnately divided.

Common Wintercress *Barbarea vulgaris* (5), with dark green shiny leaves and pods closely pressed to the stem, is misleadingly named; it flowers in May, not in winter. **Great Yellowcress** *Rorippa amphibia* (6) is a tall waterside plant with globular pods. **Creeping Yellowcress** *R. sylvestris* (7), is a low straggling plant, which usually grows on mud, and has petals longer than sepals. The more erect Marsh Yellowcress *R. palustris* has smaller flowers, the petals no longer than the sepals, and dumpier pods.

Treacle Mustard *Erysimum cheiranthoides* (8), the only crucifer with square stems, has narrow undivided leaves.
Hedge Mustard *Sisymbrium officinale* (9), a very common weed, has tiny flowers and pods closely pressed against the stem.

CRUCIFERS

Dame's Violet *Hesperis matronalis* (1), a frequent garden escape, with large fragrant flowers either deep lilac or white, originated as the violet not of a dame but of Damascus. **Cuckoo Flower** or Lady's Smock *Cardamine pratensis* (2) is one of the commonest spring flowers of damp meadows, appearing just when the cuckoo first calls. Its flowers too may be either lilac or white. **Wild Radish** *Raphanus raphanistrum* (3) is like a rather straggly Charlock (p. 24), but its flowers may be either white with lilac veins or paler yellow than Charlock.

Garlic Mustard *Alliaria petiolata* (4) which smells of garlic when crushed, is one of the commonest white-flowered spring hedge-bank plants, second only to Cow Parsley (p. 52). **Horse Radish** *Armoracia rusticana* (5) whose root makes horseradish sauce, is a frequent escape from cultivation. Its large wavy-edged dock-like leaves, up to 50 cm long, are sometimes pinnately divided.

Hoary Cress *Cardaria draba* (6) grows in clumps on waysides and waste ground. **Wild Candytuft** *Iberis amara* (7) a speciality of the Chilterns and other southern chalk hills, grows on bare patches, such as those made by rabbits in the downland turf. Its flowers may be either white or deep lilac.

Field Pennycress *Thlaspi arvense* (8) smells slightly foetid when crushed. Its name comes from the disc-like pods.

Shepherd's Purse *Capsella bursa-pastoris* (9), an abundant garden weed, flowers all the year round, and has leaves that vary widely from quite undivided to completely pinnate. Thale Cress *Arabidopsis thaliana* is a similar weed but with long narrow pods and leaves always undivided.

Hairy Bittercress *Cardamine hirsuta* (10) is intermediate between the last two, having long narrow pods but leaves always pinnate. Wavy Bittercress *C. flexuosa* has six stamens instead of four and wavy leaves, and grows in damp woods.

CRUCIFERS & MIGNONETTES

A distinctive group of crucifers grows by the sea. **Sea Kale** *Crambe maritima* (1) is a large sprawling plant, making big tufts of cabbage-like leaves on seaside sand and shingle. Its young shoots make a vegetable. **Sea Rocket** *Cakile maritima* (2) is a medium-sized plant of sandy shores, with lilac flowers. Rocket is an old name given to several kinds of crucifer, the most famous being London Rocket *Sisymbrium irio*, a relative of Hedge Mustard (p. 25), which grew abundantly in the ruins of London after the Great Fire in 1666, and still survives there in one spot today. **Common Scurvy-grass** *Cochlearia officinalis* (3) grows in saltmarshes and on sea-walls, and occasionally on banks inland, flowering from April onwards. Its upper stem-leaves clasp the stem. **Early Scurvy-grass** *C. danica* (4) is smaller, with flowers often lilac and appearing some weeks earlier. Its upper stem-leaves are stalked.

Watercress *Nasturtium officinale* (5) is the salad plant, widespread in slow-flowing fresh water. **Swinecress** *Coronopus squamatus* (6), on the other hand, as its name suggests, is fit as a salad only for pigs. It lies prostrate in paths and other well trodden places. Lesser Swinecress *C. didymus* is more erect, with a pungent smell and more feathery leaves.

The wild members of the Mignonette Family (Resedaceae), unlike the cultivated garden mignonette *Reseda odorata*, are unscented. **Wild Mignonette** *R. lutea* (7) has a floppy stance with six-petalled flowers and pinnate leaves. It grows on bare and disturbed ground, especially on limy soils. **Weld** *R. luteola* (8), a tall plant of waste places, has four-petalled flowers, and quite different narrow leaves. It was formerly cultivated for its yellow dye.

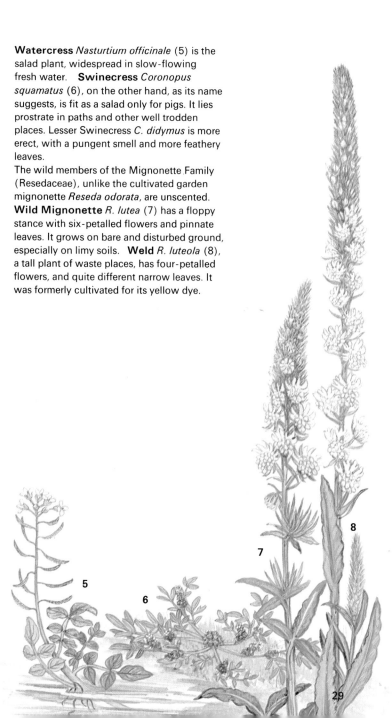

5

6

7

8

STONECROPS, SUNDEWS, SAXIFRAGES & MILKWORTS

Members of the Stonecrop Family (Crassulaceae) are mostly succulents with fleshy evergreen leaves, and open star-shaped flowers. **Biting Stonecrop** or Wall-pepper *Sedium acre* (1) is named from the peppery taste of its leaves and grows on walls and dry bare places, often on limy soils. **English Stonecrop** *S. anglicum* (2), grows in similar places, but avoids limy soils; its leaves soon turn red. **Orpine** or Livelong *S. telephium* (3), is a much taller woodland plant, whose flowers may be pink, whitish or yellow-green. **Roseroot** *Rhodiola rosea* (4), is somewhat similar, but has flowers always yellow, and grows on sea cliffs and mountain rocks. It has attractive orange fruits. **Navelwort** or Wall Pennywort *Umbilicus rupestris* (5), gets its name from its rounded leaves, which have a dimple in the middle. It grows on rocks, walls and hedge-banks, but not on limy soils. The commonest member of the Sundew Family (Droseraceae) is **Common Sundew** *Drosera rotundifolia* (7), whose rosette of long-stalked round leaves is covered with long sticky hairs. These curve inwards to trap small insects, whence the plant derives some of its nourishment. It grows only in wet bogs, heaths and moors.

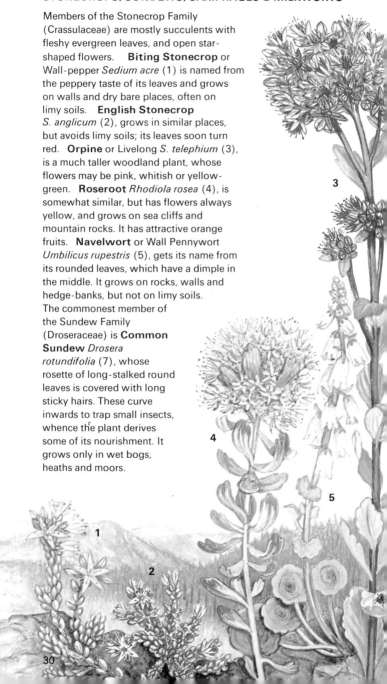

Most members of the Saxifrage Family (Saxifragaceae) grow on mountains. Two which do not are **Meadow Saxifrage** *Saxifraga granulata* (6), with flowers 25 mm across, in grassy places; and the often tiny, sometimes only 25–50 mm high, **Rue-leaved Saxifrage** *S. tridactylites* (8), whose leaves soon turn red, on walls and other dry bare places.

The graceful **Grass of Parnassus** *Parnassia palustris* (9), is in a Family of its own (Parnassiaceae), closely allied to the saxifrages. Its liking for damp grassy places, its solitary flowers and its leaf-shape all distinguish it from Meadow Saxifrage.

Milkworts *Polygala*, with their mauve, blue or white flowers, all belong to their own small family, Polygalaceae. **Common Milkwort** *P. vulgaris* (10), is the commonest and most widespread, growing in grassy places. All its leaves are alternate and scattered up the stems. Heath Milkwort *P. serpyllifolia* grows on heaths and moors, avoiding limy soils and has at least the lower leaves opposite. Chalk Milkwort *P. calcarea*, on the other hand, grows only on limy soils, and has its lowest leaves in a rosette.

6

9

8

10

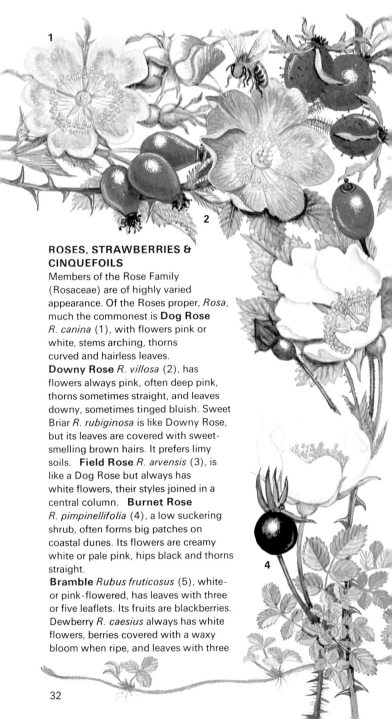

ROSES, STRAWBERRIES & CINQUEFOILS

Members of the Rose Family (Rosaceae) are of highly varied appearance. Of the Roses proper, *Rosa*, much the commonest is **Dog Rose** *R. canina* (1), with flowers pink or white, stems arching, thorns curved and hairless leaves.

Downy Rose *R. villosa* (2), has flowers always pink, often deep pink, thorns sometimes straight, and leaves downy, sometimes tinged bluish. Sweet Briar *R. rubiginosa* is like Downy Rose, but its leaves are covered with sweet-smelling brown hairs. It prefers limy soils. **Field Rose** *R. arvensis* (3), is like a Dog Rose but always has white flowers, their styles joined in a central column. **Burnet Rose** *R. pimpinellifolia* (4), a low suckering shrub, often forms big patches on coastal dunes. Its flowers are creamy white or pale pink, hips black and thorns straight.

Bramble *Rubus fruticosus* (5), white- or pink-flowered, has leaves with three or five leaflets. Its fruits are blackberries. Dewberry *R. caesius* always has white flowers, berries covered with a waxy bloom when ripe, and leaves with three

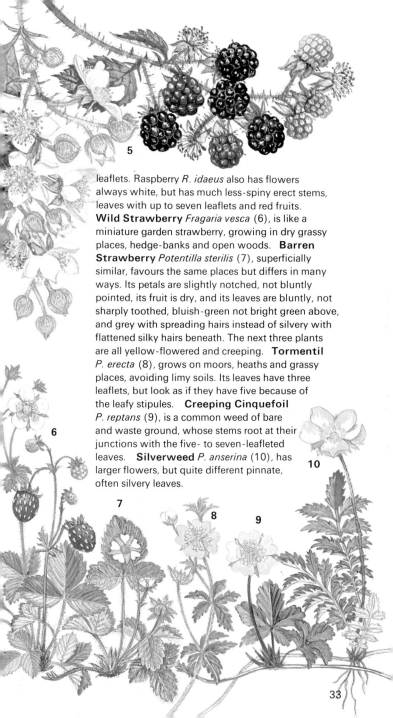

leaflets. Raspberry *R. idaeus* also has flowers always white, but has much less-spiny erect stems, leaves with up to seven leaflets and red fruits.

Wild Strawberry *Fragaria vesca* (6), is like a miniature garden strawberry, growing in dry grassy places, hedge-banks and open woods. **Barren Strawberry** *Potentilla sterilis* (7), superficially similar, favours the same places but differs in many ways. Its petals are slightly notched, not bluntly pointed, its fruit is dry, and its leaves are bluntly, not sharply toothed, bluish-green not bright green above, and grey with spreading hairs instead of silvery with flattened silky hairs beneath. The next three plants are all yellow-flowered and creeping. **Tormentil** *P. erecta* (8), grows on moors, heaths and grassy places, avoiding limy soils. Its leaves have three leaflets, but look as if they have five because of the leafy stipules. **Creeping Cinquefoil** *P. reptans* (9), is a common weed of bare and waste ground, whose stems root at their junctions with the five- to seven-leafleted leaves. **Silverweed** *P. anserina* (10), has larger flowers, but quite different pinnate, often silvery leaves.

BURNETS, MEADOWSWEET & AGRIMONY

Marsh Cinquefoil *Potentilla palustris* (1), and **Water Avens** *Geum rivale* (2), are two superficially similar plants of damp places, but the cinquefoil prefers marshes away from limy soils and the avens prefers woodlands. The cinquefoil has deep red-purple flowers, erect and star-shaped, and the end lobe of its leaves is pointed. The avens has duller pink-purple flowers, bell-shaped and nodding, which appear a month earlier, in April; the end lobe of its leaves is blunt. The very common **Herb Bennet** *G. urbanum* (3), a close relative of Water Avens, grows in drier woods and hedgebanks, and hybridises with it whenever the two grow close together.

Salad Burnet *Sanguisorba minor* (4), is one of the most characteristic plants of chalk and limestone grassland. Its tiny petalless flowers are of two sexes, in the same flowerhead, the male with yellow stamens and the female with red styles. The larger and stouter **Great Burnet** *S. officinalis* (5), grows in damp meadows, and its deep red flowers are in an oblong not a roundish head.

The fragrant **Meadowsweet** *Filipendula ulmaria* (6), is one of

our handsomest as well as one of
our commonest wild flowers,
growing in marshes and other
damp grassy places. Its leaves are
usually silvery beneath.
Dropwort *F. vulgaris* (7), is a
very similar but shorter plant that
grows in dry turf on chalk and
limestone. Its flowers are not
fragrant, but are often tinged
purple on the back of the petals.
Its leaves are much more finely
cut, with more numerous
leaflets. **Lady's Mantle**
Alchemilla vulgaris (8), could
hardly look more un-roselike,
with its clusters of tiny green
petalless flowers, coloured only
by their yellow stamens. It grows
in woods and grassy places, more
commonly in the north.
Agrimony *Agrimonia
eupatoria* (9), is one of the
commonest wild flowers of
grassy places in summer. Its fruit
appears bur-like, but does not
stick to clothing.

35

The Peaflower Family (Leguminosae) has most distinctively shaped flowers, like those of a garden pea or bean. They are five-petalled, with the broad and often erect 'standard' at the top, the two narrower 'wings' at the sides, and at the bottom the two lowest petals joined as the 'keel'. The fruit is a longish pod, again like a pea or bean.

Gorse *Ulex europaeus* (1), also known as Furze or Whin, grows abundantly on heaths, downs and sea cliffs. Its golden-yellow flowers are richly almond-scented, and appear in any month of the year, but are at their best between April and June. Its leaves are reduced to sharp spines. Two shorter species with smaller flowers, Dwarf Gorse *U. minor* with softer spines, and Western Gorse *U. gallii*, flower in late summer and autumn.

Broom *Cytisus scoparius* (2), is like a taller spineless Gorse, with trefoil leaves, growing on heaths and in open woods and avoiding limy soils.

Dyer's Greenwood *Genista tinctoria* (3), is like a miniature Broom, growing in similar places and in damp meadows but with narrow undivided leaves.

Petty Whin
G. anglica (4), smaller still and spiny, grows mainly on heaths and moors.

Meadow Vetchling
Lathyrus pratensis (5), is one of the commonest plants of grassy places. Its leaves have a single pair of narrow leaflets, and its pods are black.

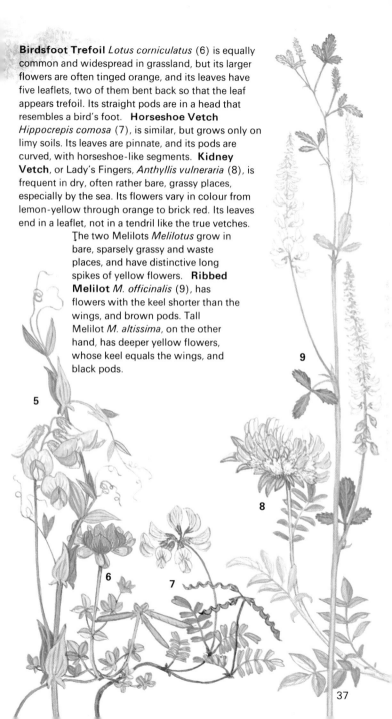

Birdsfoot Trefoil *Lotus corniculatus* (6) is equally common and widespread in grassland, but its larger flowers are often tinged orange, and its leaves have five leaflets, two of them bent back so that the leaf appears trefoil. Its straight pods are in a head that resembles a bird's foot. **Horseshoe Vetch** *Hippocrepis comosa* (7), is similar, but grows only on limy soils. Its leaves are pinnate, and its pods are curved, with horseshoe-like segments. **Kidney Vetch**, or Lady's Fingers, *Anthyllis vulneraria* (8), is frequent in dry, often rather bare, grassy places, especially by the sea. Its flowers vary in colour from lemon-yellow through orange to brick red. Its leaves end in a leaflet, not in a tendril like the true vetches.

The two Melilots *Melilotus* grow in bare, sparsely grassy and waste places, and have distinctive long spikes of yellow flowers. **Ribbed Melilot** *M. officinalis* (9), has flowers with the keel shorter than the wings, and brown pods. Tall Melilot *M. altissima*, on the other hand, has deeper yellow flowers, whose keel equals the wings, and black pods.

37

PURPLE, PINK & WHITE PEAFLOWERS

Vetches proper *Vicia* all have pinnate leaves ending with the tendrils that enable them to scramble over other plants. **Tufted Vetch** *V. cracca* (1), growing in hedges, scrub and fens, is perhaps the handsomest. It has small blue-violet flowers and brown pods. The smaller **Bush Vetch** *V. sepium* (2), also in hedge-banks, scrub and open woods, has larger blue-purple flowers appearing in late April, black pods, and fewer leaflets in each leaf. **Common Vetch** *V. sativa* (3), grows in bare or sparsely grassy places and used to be cultivated as a fodder plant. Its flowers are red-purple and are single or paired. **Wood Vetch** *V. sylvatica* (10), a local plant of open woods and near the sea, has most attractive large white or pale lilac flowers.

Smooth Tare *V. tetrasperma* (4), has small deep lilac flowers and grows in grassy places. Hairy Tare *V. hirsuta*, with smaller paler flowers and more of them in each spike, is often commoner. These are not the tares of the Bible, which are believed to be Darnel Grass, *Lolium temulentum*, a weedy relative of the Perennial Rye-grass *L. perenne* (p. 121).

White Melilot *Melilotus alba* (5), grown as a fodder crop under the name Bokhara Clover, is frequent on bare and waste ground. Its pods are brown. **Goat's Rue** *Galega officinalis* (6), is a garden escape that is widely established in waste places, especially around London. Its flowers may be either white or pinkish lilac. **Sainfoin** *Onobrychis viciifolia* (7), found in dry grassy and bare places, especially on limy soils, is still sometimes grown as a fodder crop. Its name comes from the French for 'holy hay'.

Rest-harrow *Ononis repens* (8), got its name from its tough stems, which 'arrested' mediaeval harrows. It may have soft spines. Spiny Rest-harrow *O. spinosa* has sharper spines and redder-pink flowers, whose wings are shorter than, instead of equalling, the keel. Both grow in dry grassland. **Bitter Vetchling** *Lathyrus montanus* (9), grows in woods, scrub and heaths, and its leaves end in a point, not a tendril. Its red-purple flowers, which start as early as April, soon fade blue.

39

CLOVERS, TREFOILS & MEDICKS

Clovers and Trefoils *Trifolium* and Medicks *Medicago* all grow in grassy
places and have their small flowers in dense rounded heads and their
leaves with three leaflets (trefoil). **Red Clover** *T. pratense* (1), one of
the standard fodder crops, is one of the two most abundant clovers. The
other is **White Clover** *T. repens* (3), equally widely grown as Wild White,
Dutch or Kentish Clover. Its flowers, in smaller heads may be either
white or pink. The leaves of both often bear a whitish crescentic mark.
Strawberry Clover *T. fragiferum* (2), is like a small Red Clover, but
its globular flowerheads swell in fruit to appear like miniature pale pink
strawberries. **Alsike Clover** *T. hybridum* (4), also grown for fodder,
differs from White Clover in its shorter-stalked flowers being usually pink
and its leaflets never having white markings. **Haresfoot Clover**
T. arvense (5), avoids limy soils and its flowers may be either whitish or
dirty pink.

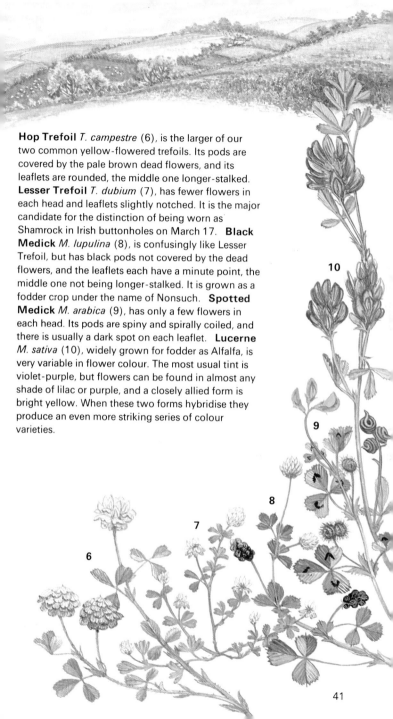

Hop Trefoil *T. campestre* (6), is the larger of our two common yellow-flowered trefoils. Its pods are covered by the pale brown dead flowers, and its leaflets are rounded, the middle one longer-stalked. **Lesser Trefoil** *T. dubium* (7), has fewer flowers in each head and leaflets slightly notched. It is the major candidate for the distinction of being worn as Shamrock in Irish buttonholes on March 17. **Black Medick** *M. lupulina* (8), is confusingly like Lesser Trefoil, but has black pods not covered by the dead flowers, and the leaflets each have a minute point, the middle one not being longer-stalked. It is grown as a fodder crop under the name of Nonsuch. **Spotted Medick** *M. arabica* (9), has only a few flowers in each head. Its pods are spiny and spirally coiled, and there is usually a dark spot on each leaflet. **Lucerne** *M. sativa* (10), widely grown for fodder as Alfalfa, is very variable in flower colour. The most usual tint is violet-purple, but flowers can be found in almost any shade of lilac or purple, and a closely allied form is bright yellow. When these two forms hybridise they produce an even more striking series of colour varieties.

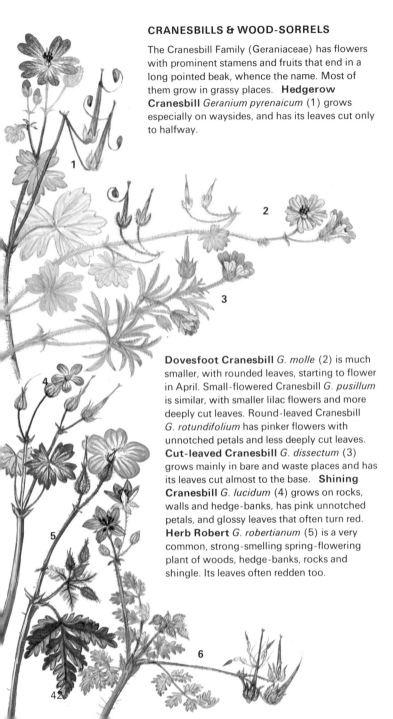

CRANESBILLS & WOOD-SORRELS

The Cranesbill Family (Geraniaceae) has flowers with prominent stamens and fruits that end in a long pointed beak, whence the name. Most of them grow in grassy places. **Hedgerow Cranesbill** *Geranium pyrenaicum* (1) grows especially on waysides, and has its leaves cut only to halfway.

Dovesfoot Cranesbill *G. molle* (2) is much smaller, with rounded leaves, starting to flower in April. Small-flowered Cranesbill *G. pusillum* is similar, with smaller lilac flowers and more deeply cut leaves. Round-leaved Cranesbill *G. rotundifolium* has pinker flowers with unnotched petals and less deeply cut leaves. **Cut-leaved Cranesbill** *G. dissectum* (3) grows mainly in bare and waste places and has its leaves cut almost to the base. **Shining Cranesbill** *G. lucidum* (4) grows on rocks, walls and hedge-banks, has pink unnotched petals, and glossy leaves that often turn red. **Herb Robert** *G. robertianum* (5) is a very common, strong-smelling spring-flowering plant of woods, hedge-banks, rocks and shingle. Its leaves often redden too.

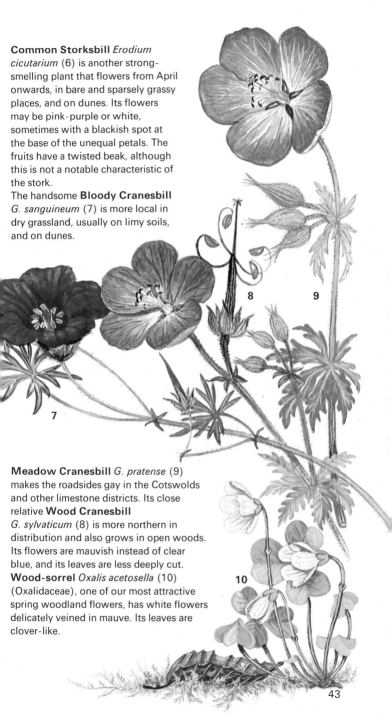

Common Storksbill *Erodium cicutarium* (6) is another strong-smelling plant that flowers from April onwards, in bare and sparsely grassy places, and on dunes. Its flowers may be pink-purple or white, sometimes with a blackish spot at the base of the unequal petals. The fruits have a twisted beak, although this is not a notable characteristic of the stork.

The handsome **Bloody Cranesbill** *G. sanguineum* (7) is more local in dry grassland, usually on limy soils, and on dunes.

Meadow Cranesbill *G. pratense* (9) makes the roadsides gay in the Cotswolds and other limestone districts. Its close relative **Wood Cranesbill** *G. sylvaticum* (8) is more northern in distribution and also grows in open woods. Its flowers are mauvish instead of clear blue, and its leaves are less deeply cut.

Wood-sorrel *Oxalis acetosella* (10) (Oxalidaceae), one of our most attractive spring woodland flowers, has white flowers delicately veined in mauve. Its leaves are clover-like.

43

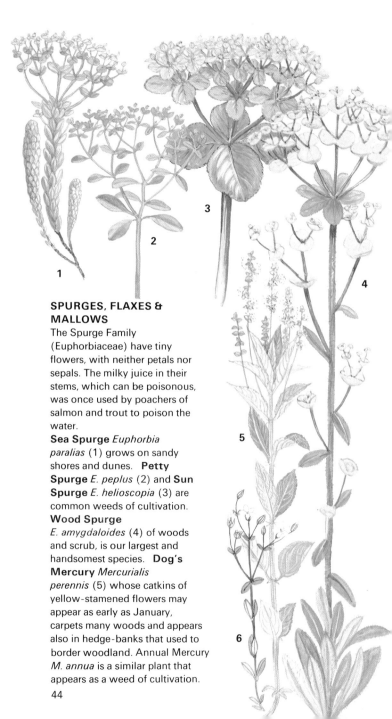

SPURGES, FLAXES & MALLOWS

The Spurge Family (Euphorbiaceae) have tiny flowers, with neither petals nor sepals. The milky juice in their stems, which can be poisonous, was once used by poachers of salmon and trout to poison the water.

Sea Spurge *Euphorbia paralias* (1) grows on sandy shores and dunes. **Petty Spurge** *E. peplus* (2) and **Sun Spurge** *E. helioscopia* (3) are common weeds of cultivation. **Wood Spurge** *E. amygdaloides* (4) of woods and scrub, is our largest and handsomest species. **Dog's Mercury** *Mercurialis perennis* (5) whose catkins of yellow-stamened flowers may appear as early as January, carpets many woods and appears also in hedge-banks that used to border woodland. Annual Mercury *M. annua* is a similar plant that appears as a weed of cultivation.

44

Purging Flax *Linum catharticum* (6) (Flax Family, Linaceae) looks like a chickweed (p. 17), but has five unnotched petals. It grows in chalk and limestone grassland. Flowers of the Mallow Family (Malvaceae) have a double ring of joined sepals. Their fruits are flat discs. **Common Mallow** *Malva sylvestris* (7) is a very common plant of roadsides and other waste places. Its leaves often have a dark spot. **Dwarf Mallow** *M. neglecta* (8) is much smaller, with paler, almost whitish flowers. **Musk Mallow** *M. moschata* (9), with its beautiful rose-pink flowers, may look like a garden escape, but it is quite wild and native. It grows in grassy places and among bushes. **Tree Mallow** *Lavatera arborea* (10) is the most upstanding species, reaching well over 2 m in height, on rocks and bare ground by the sea. Its leaves and stems are covered with soft, almost woolly down.

7

8

9

10

ST JOHN'S WORTS, ROCK-ROSE & VIOLETS

The St John's Wort Family (Guttiferae) has many-stamened yellow flowers and leaves with transparent veins. The commonest generally in dry grassy places and scrub, is **Perforate St John's Wort** *Hypericum perforatum* (1), with black-dotted petals and sepals and translucent dots on its hairless leaves. Hairy St John's Wort *H. hirsutum* has paler, sometimes red-veined flowers and downy leaves and stems. Square-stemmed St John's Wort *H. tetrapterum*, also pale-flowered but with few black dots, grows in damp places, often by fresh water.

Slender St John's Wort *H. pul-chrum* (2), the prettiest of the group, often has its deep yellow flowers tinged red beneath. It grows on heaths and in scrub and open woods, avoiding limy soils.

Marsh St John's Wort *H. elodes* (3) is rather unlike any of the others: its flowers scarcely open, and its rounded leaves are grey with long hairs. It grows in even wetter places than its square-stalked relative, usually with its 'feet wet'.

Common Rock-rose *Helianthemum nummularium* (4) (Rock-rose Family, Cistaceae) is a speciality of rocks and grassland on limy soils. Its leaves are white with down beneath.

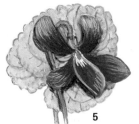

The wild members of the Violet Family (Violaceae) are recognisable by their likeness to the garden violets and pansies. **Sweet Violet** *Viola odorata* (5) is readily told by its fragrant flowers, which are almost as often white as violet-blue. It has long creeping runners, and grows in woods and especially in hedge-banks. Hairy Violet *V. hirta* differs in its unscented flowers, lack of runners, and preference for grassland on chalk or limestone.

The Dog Violets all have unscented flowers and pointed instead of blunt sepals. **Common Dog Violet** *V. riviniana* (6), with the flower spur creamy and notched, grows in woods, scrub and hedge-banks. Early Dog Violet *V. reichenbachiana* appears about a fortnight earlier, in late March, and has an unnotched violet spur. **Heath Dog Violet** *V. canina* (7), with its distinctive pale blue flowers, grows on heaths and in fens, scrub and open woods. **Marsh Violet** *V. palustris* (8) is easily told by its rounded leaves and boggy or marshy habitat.

Wild Pansy or Heartsease *V. tricolor* (9) is like a miniature garden pansy, of grassy and bare places, with flowers violet, yellow (especially on dunes) or both, and the end lobe of the leaves longer than the others. The confusingly similar Mountain Pansy *V. lutea* of hill and mountain grassland, has larger flowers with the end lobe of the leaves equalling the others. **Field Pansy** *V. arvensis* (10), a common weed of cultivation, has smaller creamy flowers, sometimes tinged yellow or violet and very variable in size.

WILLOWHERBS, LOOSESTRIFE & BALSAMS

Evening Primrose *Oenothera erythrosepala* (1), a tall garden escape widely established on waste ground and sand dunes, has crinkled leaves and stems covered with red spots.

Enchanter's Nightshade *Circaea lutetiana* (2), named after Homer's enchantress Circe, often carpets shady places and can be a tiresome garden weed. Our only two-petalled wild flower, its fruits are covered with hooked bristles. The Willowherbs proper, *Epilobium*, which make up most of the Family (Onagraceae), have four pinkish-purple petals and feathery fruits which float on the wind. They hybridise freely. **Broad-leaved Willowherb** *E. montanum* (3), the commonest of the smaller species, grows in drier shady and waste places, sometimes as a garden weed. Marsh Willowherb *E. palustre* has narrow leaves and grows in wet places. American Willowherb *E. adenocaulon*, a transatlantic invader now common on urban ground, has smaller flowers. **Rosebay Willowherb** *E. angustifolium* (4), with unequal petals, forms large patches on heaths and waste ground, and in clearings. By colonising freshly burned ground it has earned the name of Fireweed. **Great Willowherb** *E. hirsutum* (5), known as Codlins and Cream from its scent, is tall and softly hairy all over. Hoary Willowherb *E. parviflorum* is shorter with much smaller flowers.

Our commonest species of the Balsam Family (Balsaminaceae) are both introduced: the tall **Himalayan Balsam** *Impatiens glandulifera* (6) from Asia and the shorter **Orange Balsam** *I. capensis* (7) from North America. Both grow by fresh water, but Himalayan Balsam also spreads away from the waterside.

Purple Loosestrife *Lythrum salicaria* (8) (Loosestrife Family), is a tall waterside plant.

DAPHNES, UMBELLIFERS, IVY & BRYONY

Our two members of the Daphne Family (Thymelaeaceae) are both small shrubs, growing in woods on limy soils and flowering in early spring. The fragrant flowers of **Mezereon** *Daphne mezereum* (1) appear before the leaves and produce red berries. It is now distinctly uncommon, largely because so many people have dug it up for their gardens. The black-berried **Spurge Laurel** *D. laureola* (2) is in no way related to the spurges, but its leathery evergreen leaves are quite laurel-like.

Ivy *Hedera helix* (3) (Ivy Family, Araliaceae), our only climber that uses tiny roots to climb with, is also one of our very few plants not to flower till the autumn. Many people have a quite unreasoning prejudice against ivy, contending that it 'strangles' trees. There is absolutely no evidence for this.

White Bryony *Bryonia cretica* (4) (Gourd Family, Cucurbitaceae) is a climber distinguished from the totally unrelated Black Bryony (page 99) by its tendrils, larger five-petalled flowers and ivy-shaped leaves. Red-berried, it grows in hedges and scrub, mainly on limy soils.

For general details of the Carrot Family (Umbelliferae), see page 52. **Sanicle** *Sanicula europaea* (5) is an unusual umbellifer that grows commonly in woods, especially on limy soils. Its flowers grow in a tight head instead of an open umbel. The handsome **Sea Holly** *Eryngium maritimum* (6) is a similarly aberrant umbellifer. Its leaves are spiny, whence its name, and it grows on sand and shingle shores.

Four common or frequent umbellifers have yellow flowers. The strong-smelling (when crushed) **Wild Parsnip** *Pastinaca sativa* (7), the origin of the vegetable, is a tall plant of bare and grassy places, often on limy soils. **Pepper Saxifrage** *Silaum silaus* (8), another grassland plant, is neither a pepper nor a saxifrage; its leaf segments are narrow. **Alexanders** *Smyrnium olusatrum* (9), a former potherb well established on bare ground and in hedge-banks, mainly near the sea, is also strong-smelling. It has glossy leaves and black fruits. **Rock Samphire** *Crithmum maritimum* (10), used also to be eaten for its fleshy greyish leaves. It still grows widely by the sea, on cliffs, rocks and sandy shores.

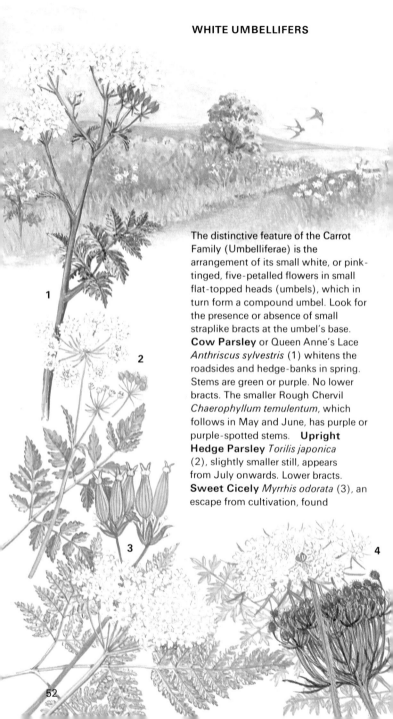

The distinctive feature of the Carrot Family (Umbelliferae) is the arrangement of its small white, or pink-tinged, five-petalled flowers in small flat-topped heads (umbels), which in turn form a compound umbel. Look for the presence or absence of small straplike bracts at the umbel's base. **Cow Parsley** or Queen Anne's Lace *Anthriscus sylvestris* (1) whitens the roadsides and hedge-banks in spring. Stems are green or purple. No lower bracts. The smaller Rough Chervil *Chaerophyllum temulentum*, which follows in May and June, has purple or purple-spotted stems. **Upright Hedge Parsley** *Torilis japonica* (2), slightly smaller still, appears from July onwards. Lower bracts. **Sweet Cicely** *Myrrhis odorata* (3), an escape from cultivation, found

especially on northern banks and
waysides, has white-flecked aromatic
leaves and long fruits.

Wild Carrot *Daucus carota* (4), the
origin of the vegetable, grows in grassy
places, especially on limy soils, and
is often fleshier by the sea. The umbel's
central flower is often red. Lower bracts,
conspicuously pinnate or three-forked.

Pignut *Conopodium majus* (5), with
finely divided leaves, grows in woods
and shady grassland. Pigs grub up its
nut-like rootstock (edible also by
man). **Burnet Saxifrage** *Pimpinella
saxifraga* (6) (neither burnet nor
saxifrage) grows in dry grassland,
especially on limy soils, and has two
kinds of leaf, the upper pinnate with
broad leaflets, the lower bipinnate with
much narrower leaflets.

Ground Elder *Aegopodium podagraria*
(7), bane of the gardener, has no
bracts. **Fool's Parsley** *Aethusa
cynapium* (8) is a much less tiresome
annual weed, easily told from true
Parsley by the bearded look of its long
upper bracts.

Shepherd's Needle *Scandix pecten-
veneris* (9), a cornfield weed, is
distinguished by its few umbel spokes
and extremely long fruits, up to 75 mm
long. Stone Parsley *Sison amomum,* a
grassland and hedge-bank plant with
very small umbels, smells unpleasant
when crushed.

WHITE UMBELLIFERS & WINTERGREENS

Hogweed *Heracleum sphondylium* (1), the commonest large wayside umbellifer from late spring onwards, grows also in other grassy places, open woods and cornfields. It can reach 3 m high. The patch-forming Giant Hogweed *H. mantegazzianum*, introduced from Asia, is much larger and stouter, growing to 5 m high, the umbels up to 50 cm across. Its leaves can be poisonous to the touch, and periodically the media raise alarms about the danger to the nation's children from the presence of this invader in waste ground where they like to play.

Angelica *Angelica sylvestris* (2), another tall umbellifer, favours damp grassy places and woods and does not flower till late summer. Garden Angelica *A. archangelica*, the source of the sweetmeat, is naturalised along the Thames near Kew.

Hemlock *Conium maculatum* (3), the slayer of Socrates, also grows in damp grassy places and by fresh water. The whole plant has an unpleasant smell, and its stems are spotted purple. The parsley-scented **Hemlock Water Dropwort** *Oenanthe crocata* (4), is equally poisonous, with wedge-shaped leaflets. It will be noted that the eating of tall white-flowered umbellifers is a potentially lethal practice.

Fool's Watercress *Apium nodiflorum* (5) is a creeping plant growing in and by fresh water. Even those liable to be fooled by the likeness of its leaves to watercress should be able to detect the difference between the flowers of the two, but they will in fact come to no harm by eating this one. Lesser Water Parsnip *Berula erecta* is larger and has leaflike bracts, often three-cleft or even pinnate.

The Wintergreen Family (Pyrolaceae) are creeping hairless evergreens. **Yellow Birdsnest** *Monotropa hypopitys* (6) is a saprophyte (a plant that feeds on rotting vegetation) with no green colouring. Its stems and scale-like leaves are yellow. Not to be confused with Birdsnest Orchid (page 109). **Common Wintergreen** *Pyrola minor* (7) grows in woods and scrub and on moors and mountains. Its flowers are somewhat reminiscent of Lily of the Valley, and may be white or pale pink. Round-leaved Wintergreen *P. rotundifolia*, with more open, purer white flowers, has more nearly circular leaves and grows especially on sand dunes.

HEATHS, CROWBERRY & SEA LAVENDERS

The Heath Family (Ericaceae) are undershrubs with narrow alternate evergreen leaves. Most familiar is **Heather** or Ling *Calluna vulgaris* (1), which carpets heaths and moorlands every August, and also grows in bogs and open woods and on mature sand dunes. **Bell Heather** *Erica cinerea* (2), with larger bright red-purple flowers that appear in May, grows on drier heaths and moors. The pink-flowered **Cross-leaved Heath** *E. tetralix* (3) prefers wetter heaths, moors and bogs. **Dorset Heath** *E. ciliaris* (4), is rarer, almost confined to heaths around Poole Harbour. A larger version of Cross-leaved Heath, it has larger more elongated brighter pink flowers and broader leaves, in whorls of three, not four. The taller **Cornish Heath** *E. vagans* (5), almost equally restricted, mainly to the heaths of the Lizard Peninsula, Cornwall, has pink, lilac or white flowers with conspicuous chocolate-brown stamens. **Irish Heath** *E. erigena* (6), taller still, reaching 2 m or more, grows almost entirely on wet moors and bogs in the west of Ireland. **Cranberry** *Vaccinium oxycoccos* (7), now becoming less common because confined to bogs, a vanishing habitat, has pink flowers with petals turned

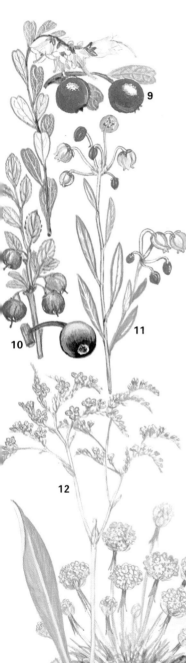

back, and produces round or pear-shaped white berries, spotted with red or brown, popular for sauces and jellies. Its leaves are whitish beneath. **Bilberry** *V. myrtillus* (10), also called Blaeberry, Whortleberry and Huckleberry, grows on moors and heaths and in dry heathy woods, and has deciduous leaves. Its fruit is a delicious black berry.

Cowberry *V. vitis-idaea* (9), with glossy evergreen leaves and an edible red berry, grows in similar places in the north. **Bog Rosemary** *Andromeda polifolia* (11), another plant of bogs and wet heaths, has pink or white flowers and leaves silvery white beneath.

Crowberry *Empetrum nigrum* (8) (Crowberry Family, Empetraceae) is a prostrate heath-like undershrub of moors and bogs. Its tiny pink six-petalled flowers produce black berries.

Common Sea-Lavender *Limonium vulgare* (12) (Sea-Lavender Family, Plumbaginaceae) carpets salt-marshes with purple every August. Its leaves have pinnate veins. Rock Sea-Lavender *L. binervosum* has shorter leaves without pinnate veins. **Thrift** or **Sea Pink** *Armeria maritima* (13) ranges from sea cliffs, rocks and salt-marshes to heaths and mountains inland. Its pale to deep pink flowers start to bloom in April.

PRIMROSES & PIMPERNELS

The well-loved **Primrose** *Primula vulgaris* (1),
most familiar of the Primrose Family (Primulaceae),
carpets woods, banks and sea cliffs in the spring,
often starting to flower in mid winter in the south.
Its leaves taper to the stalk. The fragrant **Cowslip**
P. veris (3) grows in grassy places and has a head
of deep yellow flowers and leaves that narrow
abruptly to a stalk. **Oxlip** *P. elatior* (2) carpets the spring
woods of an area of eastern England, west and south of
Cambridge. Like a large Cowslip, with primrose-coloured
flowers, it must not be confused with the primrose-cowslip
hybrid, known as False Oxlip, which has deeper yellow
flowers and more tapered leaves, and may be found singly
(never carpeting) near one or both of its parents. **Birdseye
Primrose** *P. farinosa* (4), one of the most delightful of
British wild flowers, is a local plant of damp grassy places in
the hills of the north.

Yellow Loosestrife *Lysimachia vulgaris* (5), a tall waterside plant, has its leaves often black-dotted. Similar plants in drier places are likely to be garden escapes. **Creeping Jenny** *L. nummularia* (7) has creeping stems, rounded leaves and bell-shaped flowers. **Yellow Pimpernel** *L. nemorum* (8) has star-like flowers and pointed leaves. Both grow in damp shady places.

Chickweed Wintergreen *Trientalis europaea* (9), an attractive little plant of northern moors, heaths and coniferous woods, has leaves all in a single whorl.

Scarlet Pimpernel *Anagallis arvensis* (6) called Poor Man's Weatherglass because its flowers close on dull days, is a weed of bare and cultivated ground. Its red star-shaped flowers may also be pink, lilac or blue; their blunt petals are fringed with hairs. Blue Pimpernel proper, *A. foemina*, is much less common; its flowers are always blue, with narrower-pointed hairless petals. **Bog Pimpernel** *A. tenella* (10), confined to boggy places, has delicate little pink bell-shaped flowers and rounded leaves.

PERIWINKLES, GENTIANS & BOGBEAN

Water Violet *Hottonia palustris* (1) grows in still water only, with its pinnate leaves submerged, and does not look in the least like a violet. **Sea Milkwort** *Glaux maritima* (2) is a small saltmarsh plant with small pale pink five-petalled flowers.

Greater Periwinkle *Vinca major* (3) (Periwinkle Family, Apocynaceae) is a frequent garden escape. Lesser Periwinkle *V. minor*, with smaller flowers and narrower leaves, may also grow in woods, but is probably always introduced.

Jacob's Ladder *Polemonium caeruleum* (4) (Phlox Family, Polemoniaceae), often seen in gardens, is a local native in limestone woods and grassland in the north.

The handsome **Marsh Gentian** *Gentiana pneumonanthe* (5) (Gentian Family, Gentianaceae) is the nearest we come to the magnificent gentians of the Alps. It is a decreasing plant of a decreasing habitat, bogs and wet heaths, mainly in the south.

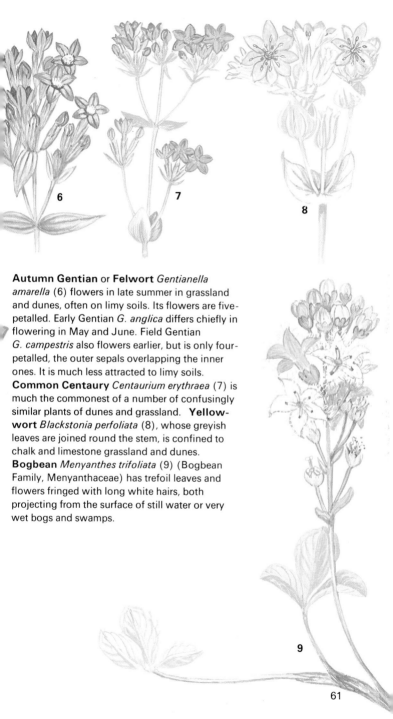

Autumn Gentian or **Felwort** *Gentianella amarella* (6) flowers in late summer in grassland and dunes, often on limy soils. Its flowers are five-petalled. Early Gentian *G. anglica* differs chiefly in flowering in May and June. Field Gentian *G. campestris* also flowers earlier, but is only four-petalled, the outer sepals overlapping the inner ones. It is much less attracted to limy soils.

Common Centaury *Centaurium erythraea* (7) is much the commonest of a number of confusingly similar plants of dunes and grassland. **Yellow-wort** *Blackstonia perfoliata* (8), whose greyish leaves are joined round the stem, is confined to chalk and limestone grassland and dunes.

Bogbean *Menyanthes trifoliata* (9) (Bogbean Family, Menyanthaceae) has trefoil leaves and flowers fringed with long white hairs, both projecting from the surface of still water or very wet bogs and swamps.

BEDSTRAWS & MADDERS

Members of the Bedstraw Family (Rubiaceae) owe their name to some, which are fragrant when dried, having been used to stuff mattresses in the Middle Ages. Their usually four-petalled flowers are in loose clusters, and their narrow leaves are arranged in whorls up the weak, straggling square stems. **Woodruff** or Sweet Woodruff *Galium odoratum* (1) is one of the species that dry fragrant. It carpets spring woodlands and has fruits covered with hooked bristles. **Hedge Bedstraw** *G. mollugo* (2) is a common plant of hedgebanks and grassland, often scrambling over bushes. Its leaves are in whorls of six to eight. Marsh Bedstraw *G. palustre* has smaller flowers, and blunter leaves in whorls of four to five, and grows in damp and wet places. **Heath Bedstraw** *G. saxatile* (3), on the other hand, also with smaller flowers and leaves in whorls of four to five, grows on dry heaths and grassland, avoiding limy soils. **Lady's Bedstraw** *G. verum* (4) has narrow dark green shiny leaves with their margins rolled back, in whorls of eight-twelve and is common in dry grassland.

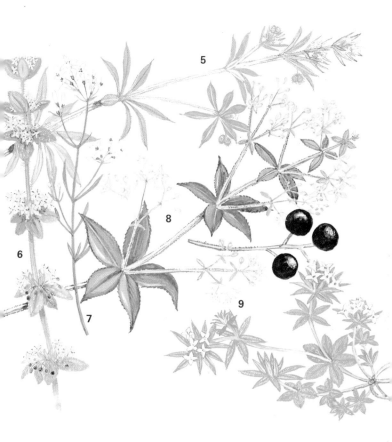

Common Cleavers or Goosegrass *G. aparine* (5) is much the commonest and most widespread member of the family, abundant in hedgebanks and on disturbed ground, including cornfields and seaside shingle. Its fruits, leaves and stems are covered with tiny prickles that cling to fur and clothing.

Crosswort *Cruciata laevipes* (6) has broader, paler, amost yellowish leaves in whorls of four, and paler yellow fragrant flowers.

Squinancywort *Asperula cynanchica* (7) is characteristic of dunes and dry grassland on limy soils, its flowers varying from pale pink to white. It owes its curious name to having been a mediaeval cure for quinsy.

Wild Madder *Rubia peregrina* (8) scrambles over other plants in woods and scrub and on rocks, mainly in the south. Its prickly dark green leaves are evergreen, and its fruit is a black berry. The Madder formerly used as a red dye was *R. tinctoria*, now only very rarely seen. **Field Madder** *Sherardia arvensis* (9) looks quite different, growing prostrate on bare and cultivated ground with tiny pale purple flowers.

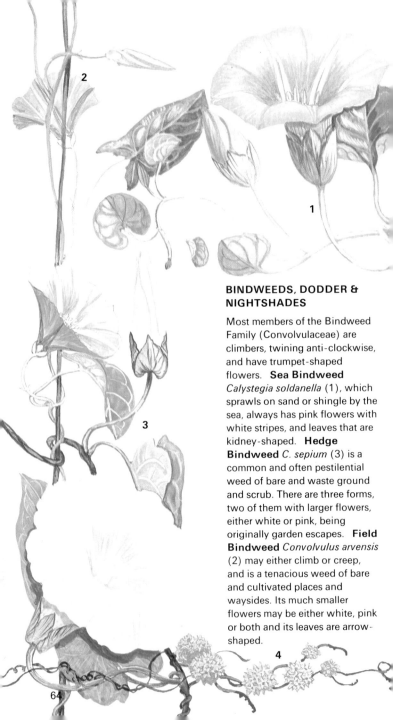

BINDWEEDS, DODDER & NIGHTSHADES

Most members of the Bindweed Family (Convolvulaceae) are climbers, twining anti-clockwise, and have trumpet-shaped flowers. **Sea Bindweed** *Calystegia soldanella* (1), which sprawls on sand or shingle by the sea, always has pink flowers with white stripes, and leaves that are kidney-shaped. **Hedge Bindweed** *C. sepium* (3) is a common and often pestilential weed of bare and waste ground and scrub. There are three forms, two of them with larger flowers, either white or pink, being originally garden escapes. **Field Bindweed** *Convolvulus arvensis* (2) may either climb or creep, and is a tenacious weed of bare and cultivated places and waysides. Its much smaller flowers may be either white, pink or both and its leaves are arrow-shaped.

Common Dodder *Cuscuta epithymum*
(4) looks like a web of red cotton
enveloping heather, gorse and other plants
of the heaths and scrub where it usually
grows. Its small, pale pink fragrant bell-
shaped flowers occur in knotlike heads
along the leafless stems.

Most members of the Nightshade Family
(Solanaceae), are poisonous. The common
Bittersweet or Woody Nightshade
Solanum dulcamara (5) clambers over
other plants in woods, scrub, hedges and
shingle. Its fruit is a poisonous berry, which
turns yellow before it ripens red.   **Black
Nightshade** *S. nigrum* (6) is a common
weed of cultivation, so named because of
its poisonous black berries.

Deadly Nightshade *Atropa belladonna*
(7), much less common than Bittersweet
with which many people confuse it, is an
erect plant that grows in woods and scrub
and among rocks on limy soils. Its large dull
purple bell-shaped flowers are quite
different. Its very poisonous black berry is
the size of a small cherry.

Henbane *Hyoscyamus niger* (8), not very
common, looks positively evil. It smells
unpleasant, is very poisonous, and is
covered with sticky hairs. Its flowers are of
a livid creamy colour unlike any others.

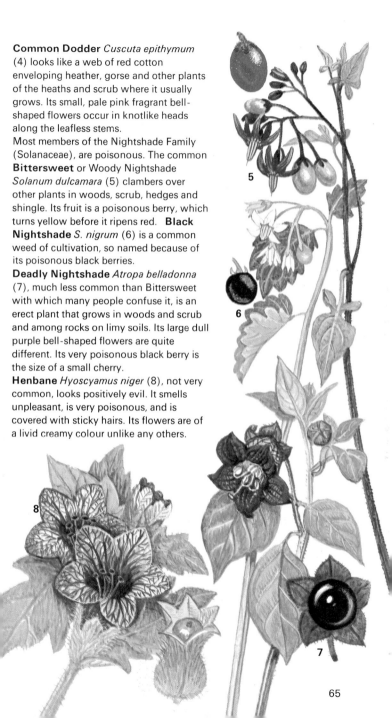

COMFREYS, BUGLOSSES, FORGETMENOTS & VERBENAS

Most plants of the Borage Family (Boraginaceae) are hairy, often roughly so. Their five-petalled flowers are often pink in bud. **Common Comfrey** *Symphytum officinale* (1), a tall marsh and waterside plant, has tubular flowers of creamy white or mauve. Its leaves run down on to the stems, as far as the next leaf-junction. **Russian Comfrey** *S. x uplandicum* (2), which grows on roadsides and waste places, has bright blue or mauve flowers, and is a hybrid of common comfrey with another species, once grown as a fodder plant. Its leaves do not run down the stems as far as the next leaf-junction.

Viper's Bugloss *Echium vulgare* (3) makes a vivid splash of blue when it grows in quantity on dunes and other dry, bare and sparsely grassy places. **Green Alkanet** *Pentaglottis sempervirens* (4) is an early-flowering, increasingly common garden escape in hedge-banks and on waysides. **Bugloss** *Anchusa arvensis* (5) also flowers from April onwards in dry, bare, often sandy or cultivated ground. **Common Gromwell** *Lithospermum officinale* (6) is a tall plant of woods and scrub, often on limy soils. Its leaves have prominent side veins which are lacking in the Corn Gromwell *Buglossoides arvensis*, a much shorter cornfield weed.

Forgetmenots *Myosotis* all have small blue flowers, appearing early, whose size is an important distinction. **Wood Forgetmenot** *M. sylvatica* (8) has sky-blue flowers 6–12 mm across and grows as a wild plant mainly in woods, but more frequently as a garden escape on waysides and waste ground. **Changing Forgetmenot** *M. discolor* (9), growing in bare places, usually on sandy soils, has creamy or pale yellow flowers that later turn blue. **Field Forgetmenot** *M. arvensis* (10) has grey-blue flowers less than 6 mm across, and is common on dry bare or disturbed ground, sandy places and dunes. Early Forgetmenot *M. ramosissima* has smaller bluer flowers and may be only 25 mm high. **Water Forgetmenot** *M. scorpioides* (11) and other marsh and waterside Forgetmenots flower later than the land species and have hairs pressed closely to the stem instead of spreading.

Vervain *Verbena officinalis* (7) (Verbena Family, Verbenaceae), a stiff plant of dry bare or sparsely grassy places, has flowers almost two-lipped.

PINK & PINK-PURPLE LABIATES

The Mint Family (Labiatae) has distinctive open-mouthed two-lipped flowers, square stems and opposite pairs of usually undivided leaves. Many are aromatic.

The strong-smelling **Hedge Woundwort** *Stachys sylvatica* (1), one of our commonest hedge-bank and wayside plants, has dark red-purple flowers and well stalked leaves. The only faintly aromatic **Marsh Woundwort** *S. palustris* (2), however, prefers damper places, often by fresh water, and has pink-purple flowers and short or unstalked leaves.

Betony *S. officinalis* (3) is not aromatic and grows in grassy and heathy places, avoiding lime. **Black Horehound** *Ballota nigra* (4) is strong-smelling and frequent on waysides and waste ground. **Red Dead-nettle** *Lamium purpureum* (5), a common weed of

cultivation, flowers through the winter. Slightly aromatic, it has nettle-like leaves. **Henbit** *L. amplexicaule* has smaller flowers and rounded unstalked leaves.
Common Hemp-nettle *Galeopsis tetrahit* (6) grows in open woods, heaths and bare places. Its flowers may also be yellow or white, and its stems are swollen at the junctions with the leaves. **Red Hemp-nettle** *G. angustifolia* (7), a weed of cultivation, has deeper pink flowers and stems not swollen at the junctions with the narrower leaves.
Wild Basil *Clinopodium vulgare* (8), only faintly aromatic, grows on dry grassland and scrub on limy soils. **Lesser Skullcap** *Scutellaria minor* (10) is rather local in damp heathy places, and has its flowers in pairs. The handsome large-flowered **Bastard Balm** *Melittis melissophilum* (9) is rather local and confined to woods and hedgebanks in the south, especially Devon and Cornwall.

PURPLE LABIATES

Mints *Mentha* are all highly aromatic, with flowers less markedly two-lipped than other labiates. They hybridise freely with each other. **Water Mint** *M. aquatica* (1) is pleasantly aromatic, with some flowers in a round terminal head, and grows in marshes and by fresh water. **Corn Mint** *M. arvensis* (2) is a weed of cultivation, also growing in bare damp places. It is rather sharply aromatic and has no terminal head of flowers. **Spear Mint** *M. spicata* (3) is a frequent escape from cultivation, being the mint of mint sauce. It is pleasantly aromatic and has a pointed terminal spike of flowers.

Common Calamint *Calamintha sylvatica* (4) has a mint-like savour and grows in dry grassland and scrub on limy soils. **Wild Thyme** *Thymus serpyllum* (5), with its own quite distinct scent, grows prostrate, often in mats, in dry grassy and heathy places and on dunes.

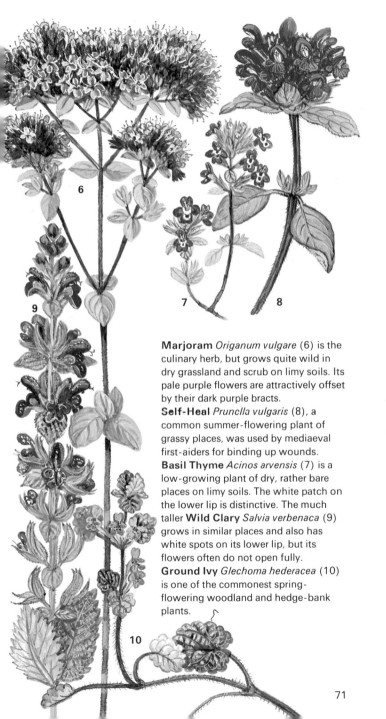

Marjoram *Origanum vulgare* (6) is the culinary herb, but grows quite wild in dry grassland and scrub on limy soils. Its pale purple flowers are attractively offset by their dark purple bracts.

Self-Heal *Prunella vulgaris* (8), a common summer-flowering plant of grassy places, was used by mediaeval first-aiders for binding up wounds.

Basil Thyme *Acinos arvensis* (7) is a low-growing plant of dry, rather bare places on limy soils. The white patch on the lower lip is distinctive. The much taller **Wild Clary** *Salvia verbenaca* (9) grows in similar places and also has white spots on its lower lip, but its flowers often do not open fully.

Ground Ivy *Glechoma hederacea* (10) is one of the commonest spring-flowering woodland and hedge-bank plants.

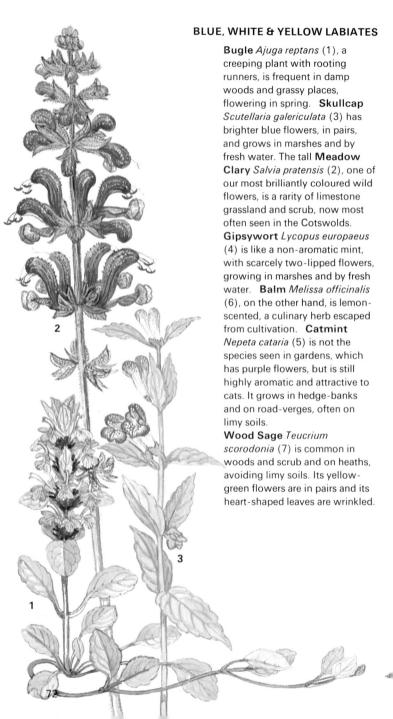

BLUE, WHITE & YELLOW LABIATES

Bugle *Ajuga reptans* (1), a creeping plant with rooting runners, is frequent in damp woods and grassy places, flowering in spring. **Skullcap** *Scutellaria galericulata* (3) has brighter blue flowers, in pairs, and grows in marshes and by fresh water. The tall **Meadow Clary** *Salvia pratensis* (2), one of our most brilliantly coloured wild flowers, is a rarity of limestone grassland and scrub, now most often seen in the Cotswolds. **Gipsywort** *Lycopus europaeus* (4) is like a non-aromatic mint, with scarcely two-lipped flowers, growing in marshes and by fresh water. **Balm** *Melissa officinalis* (6), on the other hand, is lemon-scented, a culinary herb escaped from cultivation. **Catmint** *Nepeta cataria* (5) is not the species seen in gardens, which has purple flowers, but is still highly aromatic and attractive to cats. It grows in hedge-banks and on road-verges, often on limy soils.

Wood Sage *Teucrium scorodonia* (7) is common in woods and scrub and on heaths, avoiding limy soils. Its yellow-green flowers are in pairs and its heart-shaped leaves are wrinkled.

Large-flowered Hemp-nettle
Galeopsis speciosa (8) is a weed of
cultivation and waste places that has a
purple lower lip on its pale yellow
flowers, and non-stinging nettle-like
leaves. **Yellow Archangel** *Lamiastrum
galeobdolon* (9) on the other hand, is
strong-smelling and creeps about
woods with its long runners. **White
Dead-nettle** or White Archangel
Lamium album (10) is a universal weed
of waysides and waste places that will
flower right through a mild winter. It is
faintly aromatic and its leaves are nettle-
like but do not sting.

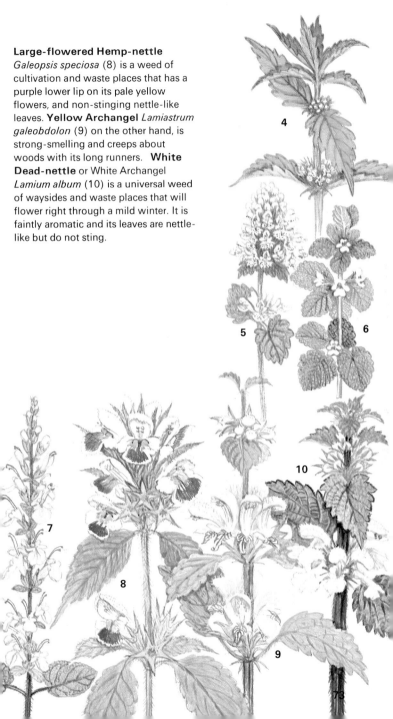

MULLEINS & SPEEDWELLS

Flowers of the Figwort Family (Scrophulariaceae) are of two quite distinct shapes, open and saucer-like as in the Mulleins and Speedwells on this page, and two-lipped, as in the Toadflaxes and others on pages 76–77. **Great Mullein** *Verbascum thapsus* (1) is a tall plant, covered with white woolly down, that grows in dry bare and grassy places and open scrub. The hairs on its stamens are white, and its broad unstalked leaves run down on to winged stems. **Dark Mullein** *V. nigrum* (2) is shorter and less conspicuously downy, growing in dry grassland on limy soils. The hairs on its stamens are purple, and its heart-shaped leaves are stalked.

Germander Speedwell *Veronica chamaedrys* (3) grows in grassy places and open scrub, and has bright blue white-centred flowers and two opposite lines of hairs on its stems. Wood Speedwell *V. montana*, of damp woods, has smaller, paler, mauvish-blue flowers, leaves purplish beneath and stems hairy all round. **Heath Speedwell** *V. officinalis* (4) grows in dry grassland and on heaths; its small flowers are lilac. **Common Field Speedwell** *V. persica* (5) is a very common weed of cultivation, flowering throughout the year. The lowest petal of its sky-blue flowers is usually white. The less common Grey Field Speedwell *V. polita* only flowers through mild winters and has smaller, darker, all-blue flowers and greyish leaves. **Slender Speedwell** *V. filiformis* (6), an increasingly common lawn weed and garden escape, has pale mauvish-blue flowers and roundish leaves.

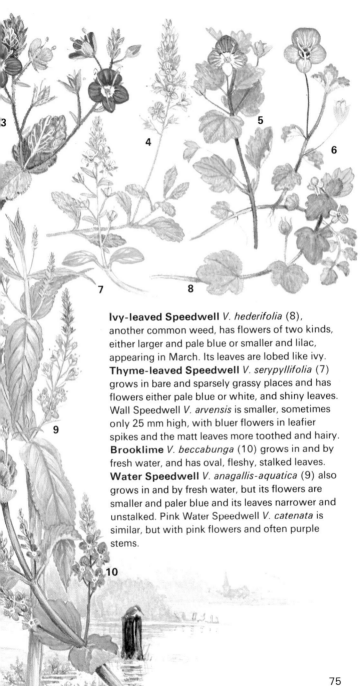

Ivy-leaved Speedwell *V. hederifolia* (8),
another common weed, has flowers of two kinds,
either larger and pale blue or smaller and lilac,
appearing in March. Its leaves are lobed like ivy.
Thyme-leaved Speedwell *V. serypyllifolia* (7)
grows in bare and sparsely grassy places and has
flowers either pale blue or white, and shiny leaves.
Wall Speedwell *V. arvensis* is smaller, sometimes
only 25 mm high, with bluer flowers in leafier
spikes and the matt leaves more toothed and hairy.
Brooklime *V. beccabunga* (10) grows in and by
fresh water, and has oval, fleshy, stalked leaves.
Water Speedwell *V. anagallis-aquatica* (9) also
grows in and by fresh water, but its flowers are
smaller and paler blue and its leaves narrower and
unstalked. Pink Water Speedwell *V. catenata* is
similar, but with pink flowers and often purple
stems.

TOADFLAXES, EYEBRIGHT & LOUSEWORT

Nos. 1–4, 6 and 9 have the lips closed; 5 and 7–10 are semi-parasitic on the roots of other plants. **Snapdragon** *Antirrhinum majus* (1) is well established on old walls and less often on rocks; also a frequent garden escape on waste ground. Its flowers are very variable in shades of red-purple, yellow and white.

Toadflaxes are miniature Snapdragons. **Common Toadflax** *Linaria vulgaris* (2) is frequent in bare and waste places. **Pale Toadflax** *L. repens* (3) is much less frequent in dry bare and sparsely grassy places. Purple Toadflax *L. purpurea*, a taller garden escape, often seen on walls, has bright violet-purple flowers. **Ivy-leaved Toadflax** *Cymbalaria muralis* (4), a creeping plant originally introduced from southern Europe in the 17th century, is now thoroughly established on walls and to a lesser extent on rocks.

Yellow Rattle *Rhinanthus minor* (5), named from the seeds rattling inside its inflated ripe fruits, grows in grasslands and cornfields. Its yellow flowers may have two purple teeth.

The two Fluellens are cornfield weeds, **Round-leaved Fluellen** *Kickxia spuria* (6) with rounded or oval and Sharp-leaved Fluellen *K. elatine* with triangular leaves.

Eyebright *Euphrasia officinalis* (7) is common in grassland, especially on downs, moors and mountains. Its white flowers vary somewhat in size, and are often tinged violet, with a yellow spot on the lower lip.

Lousewort *Pedicularis sylvatica* (8) is a squat plant of moors, damp heaths and bogs, with the upper lip of the flowers longer, and fruits inflated like Yellow Rattle. Marsh Lousewort or Red Rattle *P. palustris* is taller, with the lips of the flowers equal, and grows mainly in marshes.

Common Cow-wheat *Melampyrum pratense* (9) has flowers usually yellow but occasionally pink-purple and pairs of narrow leaves. It grows on heaths and in woods and grassland.

Red Bartsia *Odontites verna* (10) grows on waysides and other bare or disturbed ground.

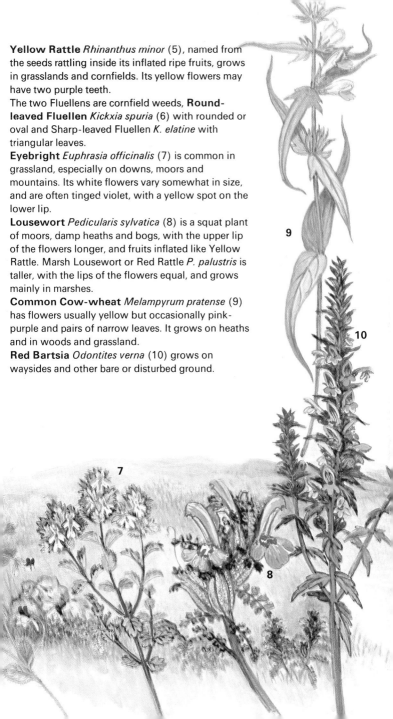

FOXGLOVE, BROOMRAPES, BUTTERWORTS & PLANTAINS

The familiar **Foxglove** *Digitalis purpurea* (1) has two-lipped flowers of a rather extreme form, almost tubular. Though widely grown in gardens, it is perfectly native in woods and scrub and on heaths, avoiding limy soils.

Monkey Flower *Mimulus guttatus* (2) is one of our gayest wild flowers, introduced from North America and widely established in marshes and by fresh water. Its bright yellow flowers have red spots on the lower lip.

Butterworts (Lentibulariaceae) grow on wet heaths, moors and bogs. Sticky hairy leaves in a basal rosette, the margins rolling inwards, entrap and digest insects. The widespread **Common Butterwort** *Pinguicula vulgaris* (4) has violet flowers with a white throat-patch, and yellow-green leaves. **Pale Butterwort** *P. lusitanica* (3), with lilac, yellow-throated flowers and olive-green leaves with red-brown veins, is found only in the west of Britain and in Ireland.

The Broomrape Family (Orobanchaceae) are parasites on the roots of other plants, lacking any green colouring matter of their own. Their two-lipped flowers are usually coloured like the rest of the plant, and their leaves are replaced by scales up the stem. They grow in grassy places and are best identified by their host plant.

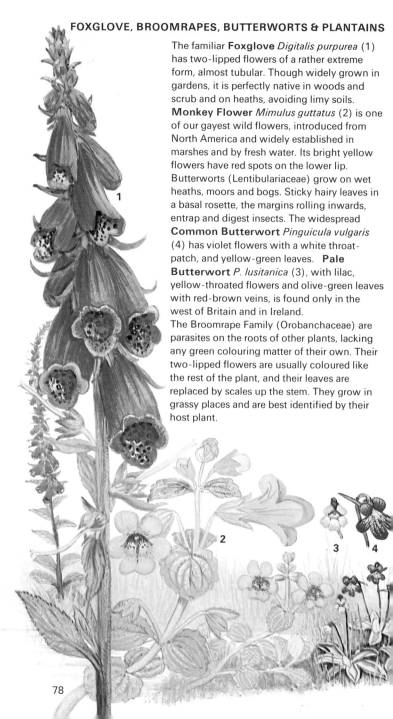

Greater Broomrape *Orobanche rapum-genistae*, from which the whole group takes its name, is rarest and 'rapes' broom and gorse. Its larger flowers have the upper lip hooded. **Knapweed Broomrape** *O. elatior* (5), usually all honey-brown, the flower's upper lip two-lobed, grows on knapweeds (page 86). **Common Broomrape** *O. minor* (6), smaller and thinner, parasitic mainly on peaflowers (p. 36) and composites (p. 84–86). Its smaller flowers can be purplish, reddish or yellowish.

Toothwort *Lathraea squamaria* (7), parasitic on Hazel, appears in spring in woods and hedges. The tiny four-petalled flowers of the Plantain Family (Plantaginaceae) are packed into a head or spike, most of the colour coming from the prominent stamens. Leaves, in a basal rosette, are strongly veined or ribbed. **Greater Plantain** *Plantago major* (8), an abundant weed of lawns and bare, well-trodden places, has green flowers and pale purple anthers which soon turn yellow-brown. **Buckshorn Plantain** *P. coronopus* (9), with yellow-brown flowers, yellow anthers, and pinnately lobed or deeply toothed leaves, grows in dry bare places, often by the sea. Sea Plantain *P. maritima*, with pinker flowers and untoothed grass-like leaves, grows only by the sea. **Ribwort Plantain** *P. lanceolata* (10), abundant in grassy and bare places, has blackish-brown flowerheads with yellow anthers. Hoary Plantain *P. media*, found on limy soils, has longer whitish spikes of scented flowers, with pink-lilac anthers, and broader leaves.

5

6

7

8

9

10

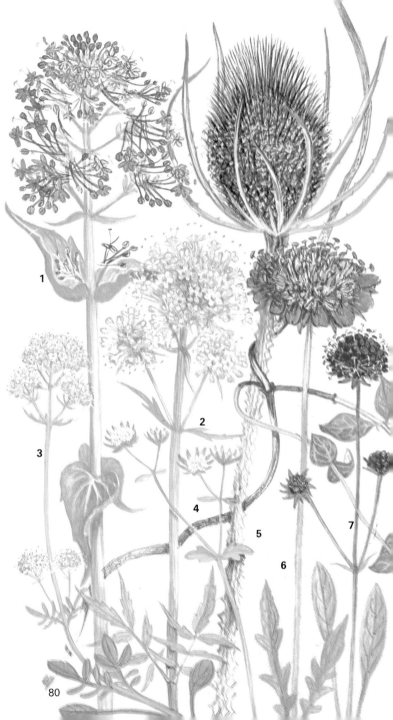

VALERIANS, TEASELS, SCABIOUSES & HONEYSUCKLES

Members of the Valerian Family (Valerianaceae) have clusters of small five petalled flowers, and pairs of opposite leaves. **Red Valerian** or Spur Valerian *Centranthus ruber* (1) has either red or white flowers and un-divided leaves. It grows widely on cliffs, rocks and walls, having been introduced from southern Europe. **Common Valerian** *Valeriana of-ficinalis* (2) is a medium-tall plant of woods and grassland, with all its leaves pinnate. **Marsh Valerian** *V. dioica* (3) is shorter, has its basal leaves undivided, and grows in marshes and fens. The diminutive **Corn-salad** *Valerianella locusta* (4) has flat-topped clusters of tiny lilac flowers. It grows on bare ground, dunes, walls and in cornfields.

The Teasel Family (Dipsacaceae) has flowerheads like those of the Com-posites (p. 84), but each floret has its own small sepal-like bracts. The leaves are in opposite pairs. **Teasel** *Dipsacus fullonum* (5) is a tall plant of bare, rather damp and sparsely grassy places. Its flowerheads are spiny, its stems and leaves are prickly, and its basal rosette of broad, white-pimpled leaves soon withers. The dead stems and flowerheads persist through the winter. **Field Scabious** *Knautia arvensis* (6), common in dry grassland and cornfields, has rather flat flowerheads, the outer ring of petals enlarged, with two rows of outer sepal-like bracts. Its leaves are pinnately lobed. Small Scabious *Scabiosa columbaria* prefers limy soils, and has dark bristles among the florets, only one row of outer bracts, and fully pinnate leaves. **Devilsbit Scabious** *Succisa pratensis* (7) grows in damper places than Field Scabious, and has more globular heads of darker blue flowers, and undivided leaves. Its name derives from the legend that the Devil, in a fit of irritation, bit off a part of its indeed truncated rootstock.

Honeysuckle *Lonicera periclymenum* (8) (Honeysuckle Family, Capri-foliaceae), is a familiar deciduous woody climber, twining clockwise, whose new leaves are among the earliest greenery in the winter woods and hedgerows. The flowers are deliciously fragrant, and the fruits are red berries. **Twinflower** *Linnaea borealis* (9), the favourite flower of the great Swedish botanist Linnaeus, is a prostrate mat-forming plant of a few coniferous woods in Scotland.

8

9

BELLFLOWERS, LOBELIAS

Members of the Bellflower Family (Campanulaceae) have undivided alternate leaves and more or less bell-shaped flowers with five petal lobes. **Harebell** *Campanula rotundifolia* (1) is perhaps the commonest, growing in dry grassland and on heaths. Its Latin name is due to its rounded root-leaves, which soon wither; its stem leaves are very narrow. In Scotland it is called Bluebell, a name reserved south of the Border for what the Scots call the Wild Hyacinth. **Clustered Bellflower** *C. glomerata* (2) is one of our most gorgeous wild flowers, with its rich violet-purple flowers. It grows on the chalk downs and other grassland on limy soils, also on dunes. **Nettle-leaved Bellflower** *C. trachelium* (3) is a medium-tall plant of woods, scrub and hedge-banks, with stems sharply angled and leaves like a stinging nettle but narrower.

Giant Bellflower *C. latifolia* (4) grows in similar places to the Nettle-leaved, but mainly in the north. It is taller, with larger flowers, bluntly angled stems and more evenly toothed leaves. **Ivy-leaved Bellflower** *Wahlenbergia hederacea* (5) is a little gem that creeps about damp woods, heaths and moors, mainly in the north. **Venus's Looking Glass** *Legousia hybrida* (6) is a cornfield weed whose dull purple flowers are often overlooked because they open only in bright sunshine. The un-stalked leaves are wavy-edged.

Sheepsbit Scabious *Jasione montana* (7) also has wavy-edged leaves, untoothed. It grows in dry grassland and on heaths, but avoids limy soils. Round-headed Rampion *Phyteuma orbiculare*, however, prefers limy soils, and has straight-edged, toothed leaves.

Heath Lobelia *Lobelia urens* (8) is a rarity of a few damp woods and heaths, not on limy soils, in southern England. The stems have acrid milky juice.

Water Lobelia *L. dortmanna* (9) is quite different, only its flower spike emerging above the surface of the hill and mountain lakes where it grows. The rosette of narrow leaves is submerged.

83

Members of the Daisy Family (Compositae), the largest plant family, are known as composites. Their small flowers are packed into a compound head, surrounded by green sepal-like bracts, which looks like a single flower of other families. The petals, joined in a tube, are either disc florets, ending in five short teeth, or ray florets, ending in a conspicuous flat flap. The flowerheads are either brush-like, with disc florets only, daisy-like, with disc florets surrounded by a ring of ray florets, or dandelion-like, with ray florets only. Fruits are often surmounted by a feathery pappus, the whole head often forming a rounded 'clock', on which they float away.

Hemp Agrimony *Eupatorium cannabinum* (1), in the tiresome way of plant names, is neither a hemp nor an agrimony, but a tall plant of damp woods, marshes and freshwater margins. **Butterbur** *Petasites hybridus* (2) grows in large patches in damp places, often by streams, and on roadsides. Its unscented flowerheads appear in spring, before the huge heart-shaped leaves, which may reach 90 cm across. **Winter Heliotrope** *P. fragrans* (3) is a garden escape, which also forms patches on roadsides and waste ground. Its smaller flowers are, however, fragrant and appear in late autumn and winter, with the much smaller leaves. **Ploughman's Spikenard** *Inula conyza* (4) is ironically named, spikenard being an old word for ointment. Another tall plant, it grows in open woods, scrub and dry grassland on limy soils. Its basal leaves are remarkably foxglove-like. **Canadian Fleabane** *Conyza canadensis* (5) is now a very widespread weed of bare and waste ground, having been introduced from North America some 300 years ago.

Mountain Everlasting *Antennaria dioica* (6) grows also on lowland heaths and moors. It is a creeping plant, with red or pink flowerheads and stems and undersides of leaves white-woolly. **Pearly Everlasting** *Anaphalis margaritacea* (7) a similar but much larger garden escape, is increasingly common on roadsides and waste ground, especially in South Wales.

Common Cudweed *Filago vulgaris* (8) grows on heaths and other sandy ground. Its flowerheads are white tipped red, but appear yellow from the tips of the sepal-like bracts. **Marsh Cudweed** *Filaginella uliginosa* (9) grows on bare damp ground rather than marshes. Both cudweeds have their stems and narrow leaves covered with silvery hairs.

DAISY FAMILY (COMPOSITES) WITH BRUSH-LIKE HEADS

Black Knapweed *Centaurea nigra* (1) grows in grassy
places and may have outer florets enlarged to appear like
rays. **Greater Knapweed** *C. scabiosa* (2), also of
grassland but only on limy soils, has outer florets always
enlarged and ray-like, with pinnately lobed leaves.
Sawwort *Serratula tinctoria* (4), like a smaller Black
Knapweed, but with pinnately lobed, saw-toothed,
spineless leaves, grows in damp grassland.
Lesser Burdock *Arctium minus* (3) grows in woods and
shady places and on waste ground; its broad heart-shaped
leaves may reach 30 cm long. The adherent burs, lasting
winter-long, are the dried flowerheads with their hooked
bracts.
Carline Thistle *Carlina vulgaris* (5) is characteristic of
dunes, chalk downs and grassland on limy soils. Its
conspicuous yellow sepal-like bracts resemble rays, but fold
up in the rain. Leaves are prickly and thistle-like. Dead plants
last through the winter.

Tansy *Tanacetum vulgare* (6), a strongly aromatic herb, well established in grassy and waste places, flowers in late summer and autumn.

Bur-marigolds, *Bidens*, grow in damp places and by fresh water, often where ponds have dried out in summer, and flower in late summer and autumn. The flattened fruits have two barbed bristles that cling to fur and clothing. **Trifid Bur-marigold** *B. tripartita* (7) has erect, occasionally rayed, flowers and narrow-stalked leaves with two lobes at the base. Nodding Bur-marigold *B. cernua* has nodding flowers and unstalked leaves with no lobes.

Mugwort *Artemisia vulgaris* (8) is a tall, slightly aromatic plant of waste ground and roadsides, once used for flavouring beer mugs, with leaves silvery beneath. Wormwood *A. absinthium*, strongly aromatic, has yellower flowerheads and whitely-downy leaves. The smaller autumn-flowering Sea Wormwood *A. maritima* of saltmarshes is silvery grey all over.

Groundsel *Senecio vulgaris* (9), an abundant weed of cultivation, flowers all year. Its flowerheads, occasionally rayed, have black-tipped bracts.

Pineapple Mayweed *Chamomilla suaveolens* (10), a pineapple-scented alien from north-eastern Asia, grows in bare, often well-trodden places.

THISTLES

Thistles have flowers of some shade of purple, with the sepal-like bracts usually spine-tipped and the pappuses not forming a clock. Their stems and leaves are usually spiny, the leaves usually pinnately lobed and wavy-edged. **Creeping Thistle** *Cirsium arvense* (1), a pestilential patch-forming weed of grassy and waste places, is only weakly spiny and has fragrant flowers. **Spear Thistle** *C. vulgare* (2), another common weed of bare and waste places, is taller and sharply spiny.

Marsh Thistle *C. palustre* (3), a tall plant of marshes and damp woods and grassland, is scarcely branched and weakly spiny, with the stalks of the flowerheads spiny. **Dwarf Thistle** *C. acaule* (4), with its basal rosette of very spiny leaves, often attacks the unwary picnicker on the chalk downs and other limy grassland. The flowerheads occasionally have short stems.

Woolly Thistle *C. eriophorum* (5) is tall, stout, very spiny and white-woolly plant of bare and grassy places on limy soils. Its globular flowerheads are 50–75 mm across.

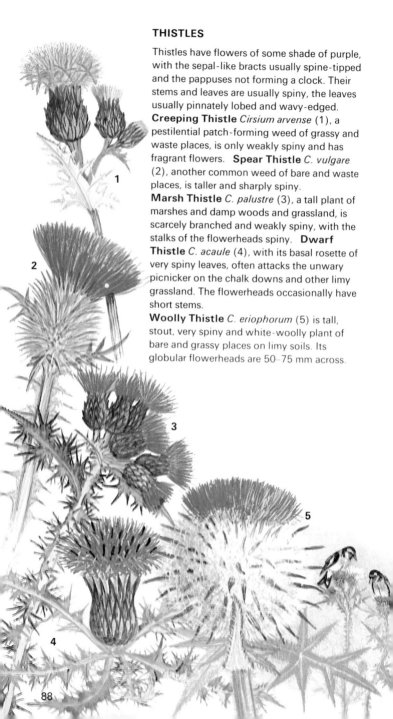

Meadow Thistle *C. dissectum* (6), a local plant of damp grassland, is scarcely spiny but cottony white all over. Melancholy Thistle *C. helenioides* is a taller, more thickly white-felted northern plant, with larger flowerheads.

Welted Thistle *Carduus acanthoides* (8), growing in hedge-banks and grassy places, is superficially like Marsh Thistle, but the stalks of the flowerheads are spineless at the tip. **Musk Thistle** *C. nutans* (10), characteristic of bare and grassy places on limy soils, is not particularly musky, but can readily be told by its large nodding flowerheads. **Slender Thistle** *C. tenuiflorus* (7), with small flowerheads, grows in grassy and waste places, often by the sea.

Cotton Thistle *Onopordon acanthium* (9) is an unmistakable plant of bare and waste ground, often on sandy soils, quite native but often also escaping from gardens. It is very spiny, with broadly winged stems, and is white all over with cottony down.

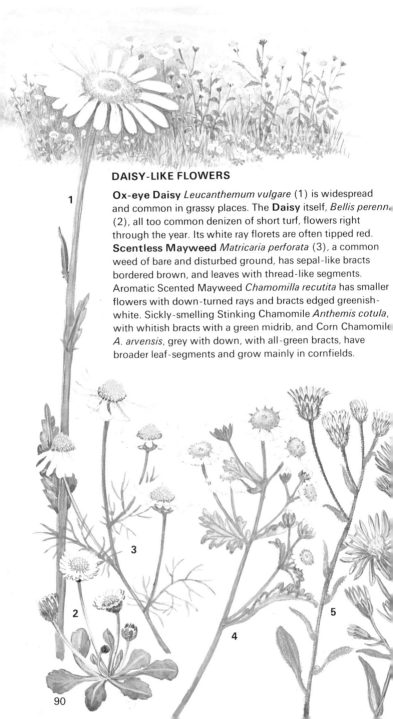

DAISY-LIKE FLOWERS

Ox-eye Daisy *Leucanthemum vulgare* (1) is widespread
and common in grassy places. The **Daisy** itself, *Bellis perenn*.
(2), all too common denizen of short turf, flowers right
through the year. Its white ray florets are often tipped red.
Scentless Mayweed *Matricaria perforata* (3), a common
weed of bare and disturbed ground, has sepal-like bracts
bordered brown, and leaves with thread-like segments.
Aromatic Scented Mayweed *Chamomilla recutita* has smaller
flowers with down-turned rays and bracts edged greenish-
white. Sickly-smelling Stinking Chamomile *Anthemis cotula*,
with whitish bracts with a green midrib, and Corn Chamomile
A. arvensis, grey with down, with all-green bracts, have
broader leaf-segments and grow mainly in cornfields.

Feverfew *Tanacetum parthenium* (4), an aromatic herb of walls and waste places has yellow-green leaves.

Michaelmas Daisy *Aster novi-belgii* (6) is a frequent and very variable garden escape to damp and waste ground, often by streams. Its ray florets may be dark or pale purple or almost white. The much smaller **Blue Fleabane** *Erigeron acer* (5) grows in dry bare and sparsely grassy places.

Ragwort *Senecio jacobaea* (7) grows commonly in dry bare and grassy places, often at rabbit warrens because rabbits will not eat it. The black and yellow striped caterpillars of the Cinnabar Moth *Hypocrita jacobaeae* are often seen on it. The end lobe of each leaf is small and blunt. Hoary Ragwort *S. erucifolius* grows in grassy places, is grey with down and has more narrowly lobed leaves, the end lobe more pointed. Marsh Ragwort *S. aquaticus* grows in damp grassland and has larger flowers and variable, sometimes undivided leaves, the end lobe large. Oxford Ragwort *S. squalidus*, an alien from southern Europe, grows on walls and bare and waste ground, flowering from April onwards; the end leaf-lobe is sharply pointed.

Common Fleabane *Pulicaria dysenterica* (8) grows in damp grassy places and has wavy-edged leaves.   **Corn Marigold** *Chrysanthemum segetum* (9), is a weed of cultivation with fleshy greyish leaves.   **Coltsfoot** *Tussilago farfara* (10) appears on bare and waste ground in late winter, well before the 5–15 cm wide leaves, which supposedly resemble the foot of a colt. Its pappuses make a clock.

YARROW, GOLDEN-RODS & SEA ASTER

The aromatic **Yarrow** *Achillea millefolium* (1) is one of our commonest grassland plants, whose feathery leaves often survive on lawns. Its flowers occasionally have pale pink ray florets. **Sneezewort** *A. ptarmica* (2) has a looser cluster of larger flowers, and undivided leaves. It is not aromatic, and grows in damp grassland and heathy places, avoiding limy soils.

Golden-rod *Solidago virgaurea* (3) is a native plant of woods, scrub, heaths and dry grassland, with a simple, flower-spike. The taller **Canadian Golden-rod** *S. canadensis* (4) is a frequent garden escape on roadsides and waste ground, with a compound flower-spike.

Shaggy Soldier *Galinsoga ciliata* (5) and Gallant Soldier *G. parviflora* are both aliens from South America that are increasing in bare and waste places, at least one of them having originally escaped from Kew Gardens. Gallant Soldier has many fewer coarse white hairs on its stems and yellower leaves.

Sea Aster *Aster tripolium* (6), common in saltmarshes, has flowerheads of two distinct kinds, daisy-like, with yellow disc florets and pale purple ray florets (like its relative Michaelmas Daisy p. 91), and brush-like, with yellow disc florets only, and so perhaps confusable with one of the Bur Marigolds (p. 87).

Golden Samphire *Inula crithmoides* (7) is a rather local plant of cliffs, shingle and saltmarshes. It too, like so many seaside plants, has fleshy leaves.

7

BLUE & YELLOW DANDELION-LIKE FLOWERS

The flowerheads of these members of the Daisy Family have ray florets only, usually in a loose cluster. Leaves usually pinnately lobed. Stems of Nos. 1–4, 6 and 7 have milky juice. **Chicory** or Succory *Cichorium intybus* (5) has bright blue flowerheads and grows in bare and sparsely grassy places. **Blue Sow-thistle** *Cicerbita macrophylla* (6) is a tall patch-forming garden escape, with mauvish-blue flowerheads, increasing on roadsides and waste ground.

Sow-thistles *Sonchus* are common weeds of bare and waste ground, with softly spiny leaves. **Perennial Sow-thistle** *S. arvensis* (2) is tall and patch-forming, often growing in cornfields. Its flowerheads are rich-yellow, and its leaves greyish beneath.

Smooth Sow-thistle *S. oleraceus* (3) has smaller, paler flowers and leaves, that clasp the stem with arrow-shaped points. Prickly Sow-thistle *S. asper* differs in having spinier leaves, often undivided, that clasp the stem with rounded lobes.

Goatsbeard *Tragopogon pratensis* (4), common in grassy places, has grass-like leaves. Its solitary flowerheads, with their projecting sepal-like bracts, open fully only on sunny mornings, earning the plant its folk name of Jack-go-to-bed-at-noon.

Wall Lettuce *Mycelis muralis* (1) grows in woods and on walls and rocks. Its small flowerheads have only five florets, and the end lobe of the leaves is triangular and sharply cut.   **Prickly Lettuce** *Lactuca serriola* (7), a tall foetid plant of bare and waste ground, has equally small flowerheads and greyish leaves that are prickly on the midrib beneath.

Nipplewort *Lapsana communis* (8), very common in shady, bare and waste places, has broad leaves often lobed at the base. Its small flowers often fail to open in dull weather.

Mouse-ear Hawkweed *Hieracium pilosella* (9) is a creeping plant of grassy and bare places, whose lemon-yellow flowerheads are often tinged red beneath the outer florets. Its leafy runners and undivided leaves are white-hairy.

Orange Hawkweed *H. aurantiacum* (10) is a frequent garden escape, also known as Fox and Cubs and Grim the Collier. Its stems and undivided leaves are black-hairy.

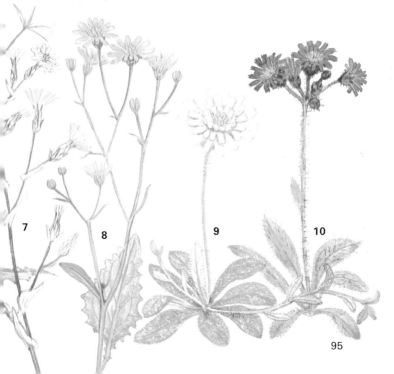

7   8   9   10

YELLOW DANDELION-LIKE FLOWERS

The pappuses of these flowers usually make a clock. **Dandelion** *Taraxacum officinale* (1), an abundant and very variable weed of bare and grassy places, flowers almost all seasons, but especially in spring. Its leaves and leafless stems have milky juice.

Common Catsear *Hypochaeris radicata* (2) of drier grassy places, flowers from May onwards. Its leafless stems have a few scale-like bracts, and its rosette of hairy leaves have blunt end lobes. **Autumn Hawkbit** *Leontodon autumnalis* (3) has a loose cluster of smaller flowerheads, appearing from July, the scale-like bracts mainly at the top of the stalk, and the end lobe of the shiny hairless leaves pointed.

Rough Hawkbit *L. hispidus* (4), of grassland on limy soils, has solitary flowerheads on leafless and bractless stalks, outer florets often red beneath, and shaggy-haired stems and leaves.

Lesser Hawkbit *L. taraxacoides* (5) much smaller and less hairy, has outer florets grey-violet beneath, and often grows on dunes.

Hawksbeards can be told by their short and spreading outer row of sepal-like bracts. **Smooth Hawksbeard** *Crepis capillaris* (6), common in grassy and waste places, has shiny leaves, the upper clasping the stem with arrow-shaped points. The taller, earlier-flowering **Beaked Hawksbeard** *C. vesicaria* (7) of similar habitat has pointed-lobed leaves clasping the stem.

Common Hawkweed *Hieracium murorum* (8) is an extremely variable plant of grassy and bare places, heaths, walls, rocks and mountains. Its unbranched, sometimes almost leafless stems have milky juice. Leaves are undivided, often toothed and occasionally blotched purple; pappuses usually pale brown.

Hawkweed Ox-tongue *Picris hieracioides* (9) usually found in grassland on limy soils, has black-haired sepal-like bracts, branched stems, wavy-edged leaves, and creamy white pappuses.

Bristly Ox-tongue
P. echioides (10), of hedge-banks and rough grassy places, has white pimples all over its roughly bristly, undivided, wavy-edged leaves and broadly triangular sepal-like bracts.

WATER-PLANTAINS, ARROWHEADS & FROGBIT

These and the following twelve pages cover the Monocotyledons, plants distinguished from the others in this book (the Dicotyledons) mainly by having only one, instead of two seed-leaves (cotyledons). The monocots also have mature leaves that are usually narrow and unstalked, often parallel-sided and nearly always parallel-veined (like the grasses, which are typical monocots); their flower-parts are in threes or sixes. The mature leaves of the dicots, on the other hand, are usually broad, often stalked, and nearly always net-veined; their flower-parts are usually in fours or fives.

The Water-plantain Family (Alismataceae) has three-petalled flowers and is found in or by fresh water. **Common Water-plantain** *Alisma plantago-aquatica* (1) is a medium-tall plant with flowers faintly tinged lilac-pink, and broad plantain-like leaves. **Lesser Water-Plantain** *Baldellia ranunculoides* (2), is much shorter, with smaller, pinker flowers, and a preference for peaty soils. **Arrowhead** *Sagittaria sagittifolia* (4) is tall with strikingly purple-spotted flowers and distinctively arrow-shaped leaves which, however, become oval when floating on water, and long trailing ribbons when submerged.

Flowering-rush *Butomus umbellatus* (3) (Butomaceae) is one of the most handsome of waterside plants, with its head of bright pink six-petalled flowers. Its fruits are purple and egg-shaped, and its three-cornered leaves long and rush-like.

Frogbit *Hydrocharis morsus-ranae* (Frogbit Family, Hydrocharitaceae) (6) is free-floating with both its flowers and its bronzy-green kidney-shaped leaves floating on the surface.

Water Soldier *Stratiotes aloides* (5) is a most odd plant, lying on the bottom of ponds during the winter, but later rising to the surface to reveal its flowers in the centre of an erect rosette of narrow spine-toothed leaves.

6

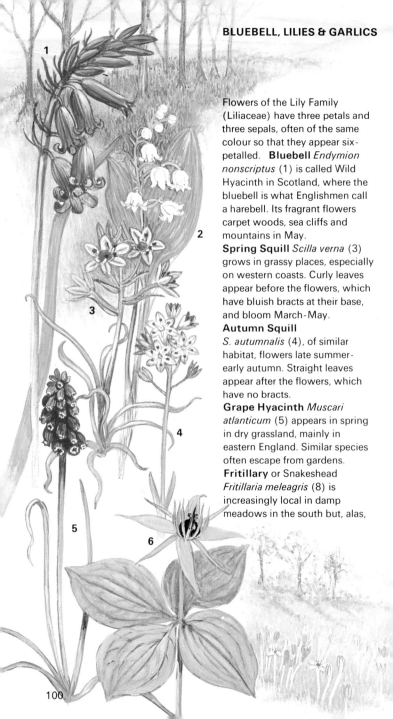

BLUEBELL, LILIES & GARLICS

Flowers of the Lily Family
(Liliaceae) have three petals and
three sepals, often of the same
colour so that they appear six-
petalled. **Bluebell** *Endymion
nonscriptus* (1) is called Wild
Hyacinth in Scotland, where the
bluebell is what Englishmen call
a harebell. Its fragrant flowers
carpet woods, sea cliffs and
mountains in May.

Spring Squill *Scilla verna* (3)
grows in grassy places, especially
on western coasts. Curly leaves
appear before the flowers, which
have bluish bracts at their base,
and bloom March-May.

Autumn Squill
S. autumnalis (4), of similar
habitat, flowers late summer-
early autumn. Straight leaves
appear after the flowers, which
have no bracts.

Grape Hyacinth *Muscari
atlanticum* (5) appears in spring
in dry grassland, mainly in
eastern England. Similar species
often escape from gardens.

Fritillary or Snakeshead
Fritillaria meleagris (8) is
increasingly local in damp
meadows in the south but, alas,

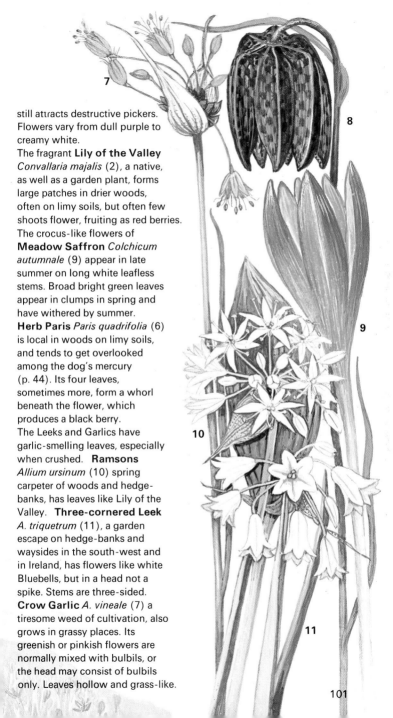

still attracts destructive pickers. Flowers vary from dull purple to creamy white.

The fragrant **Lily of the Valley** *Convallaria majalis* (2), a native, as well as a garden plant, forms large patches in drier woods, often on limy soils, but often few shoots flower, fruiting as red berries.

The crocus-like flowers of **Meadow Saffron** *Colchicum autumnale* (9) appear in late summer on long white leafless stems. Broad bright green leaves appear in clumps in spring and have withered by summer.

Herb Paris *Paris quadrifolia* (6) is local in woods on limy soils, and tends to get overlooked among the dog's mercury (p. 44). Its four leaves, sometimes more, form a whorl beneath the flower, which produces a black berry.

The Leeks and Garlics have garlic-smelling leaves, especially when crushed. **Ramsons** *Allium ursinum* (10) spring carpeter of woods and hedge-banks, has leaves like Lily of the Valley. **Three-cornered Leek** *A. triquetrum* (11), a garden escape on hedge-banks and waysides in the south-west and in Ireland, has flowers like white Bluebells, but in a head not a spike. Stems are three-sided. **Crow Garlic** *A. vineale* (7) a tiresome weed of cultivation, also grows in grassy places. Its greenish or pinkish flowers are normally mixed with bulbils, or the head may consist of bulbils only. Leaves hollow and grass-like.

101

SNOWDROP, DAFFODIL, CUCKOO PINT & BLACK BRYONY

Snowdrop *Galanthus nivalis* (Daffodil Family, Amaryllidaceae) (1) is doubtfully native in damp woods and by streams, and certainly a garden escape on roadsides and waste ground. The flowers are solitary, their inner petals tipped green. **Summer Snowflake** *Leucojum aestivum* (2) is local in damp grassland, usually near fresh water, in the south. Its flowers are in small clusters, the outer petals tipped green. Despite its name, it flowers in April and May, the distinction being from the much rarer Spring Snowflake *L. vernum*, which appears in February and March. **Wild Daffodil** *Narcissus pseudonarcissus* (3). Genuine natives grow, often in large colonies, in woods and grassland mainly in the south and west. Odd plants seen on waysides and waste ground are likely to be garden escapes.

The Iris Family (Iridaceae) has characteristically sword-shaped leaves. **Yellow Iris** or Yellow Flag *Iris pseudacorus* (5) is a common tall marsh and waterside plant with large yellow flowers, shaped like those of garden irises.

Stinking Iris or Gladdon *I. foetidissima*
(6) is rather local, in woods and scrub
and on sea cliffs. Its somewhat smaller
grey-purple flowers produce bright
orange seeds, revealed when the fruits
split in autumn. The dark green leaves
smell sickly sweet when crushed, giving
rise to a folk-name Roast Beef Plant,
which must indicate that much medieval
beef was eaten when the meat was
already starting to decay.

Wild Gladiolus *Gladiolus illyricus* (7)
is very local in scrub, grassland and
heaths, especially in the New Forest in
Hampshire, where the bright purple-red
flowers blooming in July, are often
hidden under bracken. Similar plants
flowering earlier on waysides or
cultivations in the south-west, are likely
to be Jack *G. byzantinus* escaped from
cultivation.

Montbretia *Crocosmia x
crocosmiiflora* (9) a man-made hybrid
originally raised in France a century ago,
is now widespread as a garden escape,
especially on sea cliffs in the south-
west. It is one of our few orange-
coloured wild flowers.

Black Bryony *Tamus communis* (8)
(Yam Family, Dioscoreaceae), a
clockwise-climbing native of wood,
scrub and hedges, unlike the totally
unrelated White Bryony (p. 50), has no
tendrils. Tiny, yellow-green six-petalled
flowers in loose spikes flower May-
August; red berries.

Lords and Ladies, Cuckoo Pint or
Wild Arum *Arum maculatum* (4) (Arum
Family, Araceae) grows in woods and
on shady banks. Dark green leaves,
often spotted, bluntly arrow-shaped, all
come from the roots. A dense whorl of
tiny flowers is topped by a purple,
finger-like spadix, all enveloped by a
hooded spathe hiding the flowers;
bright orange berries.

ORCHIDS

The Orchid Family (Orchidaceae) is hard to define for the layman, so that other two-lipped flowers are liable to be confused with them. Constant characteristics are that they are unbranched, usually hairless, with leaves undivided, untoothed, often narrow, keeled and rather fleshy. The flowers, usually arranged in a spike, each with a more or less leaflike bract at its base, are three-petalled, the lower usually making a distinct lip, which is often spurred, sepals often coloured so that they look six-petalled.

Pyramidal Orchid *Anacamptis pyramidalis* (1) grows in dry grassland and dunes, usually on limy soils, its very long-spurred flowers, varying from bright pink to pink-purple, in a rather flattened pyramidal spike.

Fragrant Orchid *Gymnadenia conopsea* (5) often grows with it, but also in damper grassland. It has an elongated spike of more fragrant, pale pink-purple flowers, with an even longer spur.

Autumn Lady's Tresses *Spiranthes spiralis* (9), growing in dry grassland, has a basal rosette of leaves that wither before the twisted spike of fragrant unspurred flowers with a greenish lower lip appears. **Creeping Lady's Tresses** *Goodyera repens* (2) differs in growing in woods, mainly coniferous, in hill districts in the north, and in its basal rosette of leaves still being there when the all-white flowers appear.

Bee Orchid *Ophrys apifera* (6) grows in chalk and limestone grassland, also on dunes. Flowers have pink sepals, green upper petals and a red-brown lip that looks like the rear of a small bumblebee, a pattern evolved to attract such bees. The similar but much more local **Early Spider Orchid** *O. sphegodes* (7) has green sepals and an X- or H-shaped mark on the lip. Very similar, but in miniature, the **Fly Orchid** *O. insectifera* (8) grows in grassland and open woods on limy soils. Its two very narrow upper petals make the antennae of the 'fly' and the lower lip divides to make 'arms' and 'legs'.

Early Purple Orchid *Orchis mascula* (4) generally our commonest wild orchid, apart from Twayblade (p. 106), which many do not realise is an orchid, has long-spurred flowers of varying pink-purple, and leaves usually dark-spotted. It is most likely to be confused with **Green-winged Orchid** *O. morio* (3), which also grows in grassland, and scrub but unlike the Early Purple is rare in woods. Its flowers are even more variable in colour, with distinctive green-veined sepals. Leaves are unspotted.

Burnt Orchid *O. ustulata* (10) is an attractive little plant of chalk and limestone grassland, with the lip lobed to make a manikin's arms and legs.

ORCHIDS

Musk Orchid *Herminium monorchis* (2), a diminutive plant of southern chalklands, has honey-scented flowers. The even smaller **Bog Orchid** *Malaxis paludosa* (1) grows only among sphagnum moss in bogs; its leaves are often edged by tiny bulbils.

Frog Orchid *Coeloglossum viride* (7) is probably the hardest to find of all the commoner orchids. Its yellow-green flowers (supposedly resembling a jumping frog) are well camouflaged in the short turf in which they usually grow, even when tinged red-brown. The somewhat similar Lesser Twayblade *Listera cordata*, a speciality of northern moors and coniferous woods, has the middle lobe of its lip forked and a single pair of shiny heart-shaped leaves. **White Frog Orchid** *Pseudorchis albida* (3) bears even less likeness to a jumping frog and is confined to grassland in hill districts, mainly in the north.

Butterfly Orchids *Plantanthera* grow in woods, scrub and grassland, and have vanilla-scented flowers, the lip long, narrow and long-spurred, and a pair of broad shiny basal leaves. **Greater Butterfly Orchid** *P. chlorantha* (5), generally more common, has its pollen-masses (in the centre of the flower) diverging at an angle. Lesser Butterfly Orchid *P. bifolia*, which also grows on moors and in marshes, has parallel pollen-masses.

Common Twayblade *Listera ovata* (4) frequent in woods, scrub and grassland, is often overlooked, for its unspurred yellow-green flowers with forked lip are far from conspicuous. It has a single pair of broad basal leaves like the Butterfly Orchids (hence its name), but they are matt and there are none up the stems.

Man Orchid *Aceras anthropophorum* (8) grows on grassland and open scrub on limy soils, mainly in the south. The flowers, which may be tinged red-brown, have a very distinctly manikin-type lower lip.

Early Marsh Orchid *Dactylorhiza incarnata* (9) starts to flower in May, in damp grassland and marshes. Its exceptionally variable flowers can be pink, purple, brick-red, yellow or white; the sides of the three-lobed lip soon fold back to make it appear very narrow. Leaves are yellowish-green, and unspotted, except when there is some hybridisation with Common Spotted Orchid.

Southern Marsh Orchid *D. praetermissa* (6) does not bloom till June. Its flowers are almost always pink-purple with their lip scarcely three-lobed and remaining broad. Leaves are darker green. Northern Marsh Orchid *D. purpurella*, its northern counterpart, has deeper red-purple flowers and the lip sometimes completely unlobed. **Common Spotted Orchid** *D. fuchsii* (10) grows in grassland and open scrub on limy soils. Flowers with a markedly three-lobed lip vary from pink-purple to white. Leaves are spotted purple-black. Heath Spotted Orchid *D. maculata* grows mainly on heaths and moors, avoiding limy soils, and has a much less clearly three-lobed lip.

1

2

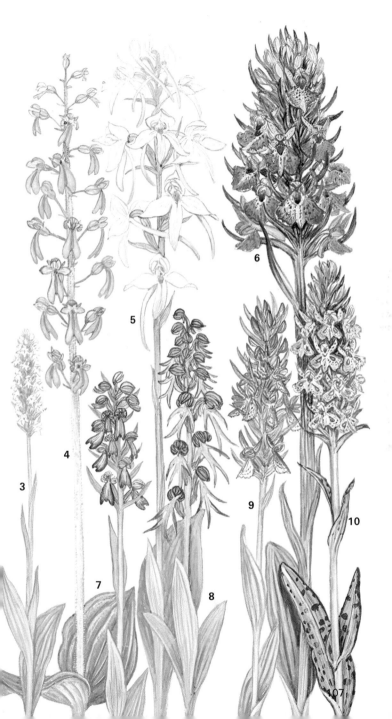

White Helleborine *Cephalanthera damasonium* (1) grows in woods, mainly of beech, on chalk and limestone. Its leafy spike of creamy white flowers scarcely open to show the yellow base of the lip. The much less common but more widespread Narrow-leaved Helleborine *C. longifolia* has a leafless spike of purer white flowers opening more widely to show an orange spot on the lip, and narrower leaves.

Violet Helleborine *Epipactis purpurata* (2) grows in woods, often of beech, but where the soil has some clay admixture. Its flowers, which appear late, in August, are purple-green outside and greenish white inside, with a purer white lip mottled violet. The narrow leaves are spirally arranged up the stems, which usually grow in a clump, and both are purple-tinged.

Broad-leaved Helleborine *E. helleborine* (3) growing in woods and on dunes, has very variable flowers, from yellow-green to red-purple, with the point at the tip of the lip turned back. Its broad leaves alternate spirally up the stem and are often tinged purple. Narrow-lipped Helleborine *E. leptochila*, a speciality of Chiltern beechwoods, has greenish-yellow flowers, with the lip remaining pointed, and two rows of yellow-green leaves up the stems.

Dark Red Helleborine *E. atrorubens* (4) has a wide range of habitats on northern and western limestone, woods, scrub, grassland, rocks and screes. Its flowers are always dark red-purple, and its leaves in two rows up the stem.

Marsh Helleborine *E. palustris* (7) grows in marshes and fens. Its attractive flowers have one of the most complex colour patterns of any of our wild flowers, with purple-brown sepals, red and white petals, and a distinctive white lip, streaked red with a yellow spot and a frilly margin.

Birdsnest Orchid *Neottia nidus-avis* (5), so named from the shape of its rootstock, is a saprophyte, devoid of green colouring matter, and feeding on rotting vegetation with the aid of a fungus partner, in shady woods, mainly of beech. The whole plant is coloured honey-brown, and has no proper leaves.

The much smaller **Coralroot Orchid** *Corallorhiza trifida* (6) is another saprophyte, growing in woods, mainly coniferous, scrub and damp places on dunes in the north. It also has no proper leaves, and its flowers vary from yellow-green to very pale yellow.

7

THE RAREST ORCHIDS

Lady Orchid *Orchis purpurea* (1) is the most magnificent of the orchids with a manikin-type lower lip, lobed to make 'arms' and 'legs'. Unfortunately it is only to be seen in woods and scrub on the chalk in Kent and eastern Surrey.

Red Helleborine *Cephalanthera rubra* (2) now grows only in one or two Cotswold beechwoods and one in the Chilterns. Its bright pink-purple flowers do not open widely, and its narrow leaves are tinged purple.

Late Spider Orchid *Ophrys fuciflora* (3), is like a Bee Orchid (p. 104) but with both petals and sepals pink and an H-shaped mark on the lower lip like the Early Spider Orchid. It is confined to chalk turf in East Kent.

Military Orchid *Orchis militaris* (4) is like Lady Orchid but with the colouring reversed, the lip darker than the hood. Once locally not uncommon, it now survives only in a handful of localities in the Chilterns and Suffolk, in woods and scrub. **Monkey Orchid** *O. simia* (6) is a miniature Military Orchid, the manikin being much more slender, now found in chalk turf and scrub only in Kent and the Chilterns.

Lady's Slipper *Cypripedium calceolus* (5) is the rarest, the most handsome and the most unmistakable British orchid, now alas, surviving in only a single locality in Yorkshire.

Irish Lady's Tresses *Spiranthes romanzoffiana* (7) used to be found in Ireland only, but has recently spread to western Scotland and Dartmoor. Its habitat of bogs and wet peaty places is a good distinction from its relatives on p. 104; another is its lack of a basal rosette of leaves.

Lizard Orchid *Himantoglossum hircinum* (8), a plant of grassland, scrub and dunes, now almost confined to Kent, has the most remarkable strap-like lip, up to 50 mm long, supposedly the body of the lizard. It can smell strongly of billy goat.

Fen Orchid *Liparis loeselii* (9) is a speciality of a few marshes, fens and dunes in East Anglia and South Wales. The undivided lip is twisted round to appear erect.

Ghost Orchid *Epipogium aphyllum* (10) is extremely hard to find in the few Chiltern beechwoods where it still grows. Being a saprophyte (see under Birdsnest Orchid, p. 109), it has neither leaves nor green colouring matter, so that the low-growing pale mauvish-yellow flowers are almost invisible against the dead leaves in the dimness of the very shady spots it favours.

RUSHES, BUR-REEDS, HORSETAILS & REEDMACES

The Rush Family (Juncaceae) are small-flowered grass- or sedge-like plants, usually of damp places, mostly erect and tufted with three sepals resembling their three petals. Rushes *Juncus* are hairless. **Soft Rush** *J. effusus* (1) has no leaves. **Compact Rush** *J. subuliflorus* (2) has stems ridged and flowerheads always compact. **Hard Rush** *J. inflexus* (3) has stiff, hard stems. **Jointed Rush** *J. articulatus* (4) has jointed leaves and blunt fruits. **Sharp-flowered Rush** *J. acutiflorus* (5) is similar but with pointed fruits. **Heath Rush** *J. squarrosus* (6), rigid and wiry, grows on heaths and moors. **Toad Rush** *J. bufonius* (7), straggly and grass-like, has green flowers. Wood-rushes have white-haired stems. The tallest, **Great Woodrush** *Luzula sylvatica* (8), grows in damp woods, especially in the west. **Field Wood-rush** *L. campestris* (9) is common in dry grassy places. **Heath Wood-rush** *L. multiflora* (10)

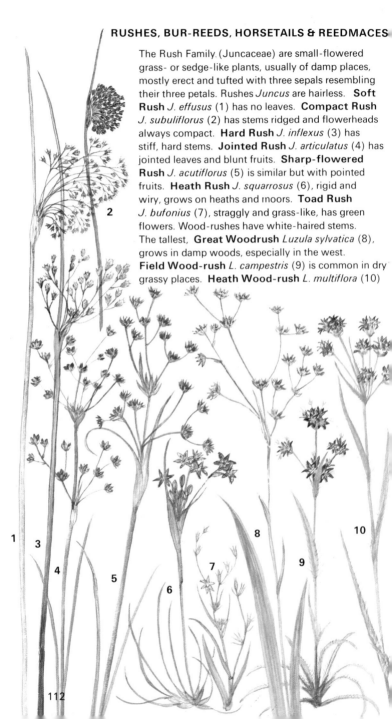

is taller, may have compact flowerheads and grows on acid soils, in woods and on heaths and moors.

Bur-reeds (Sparganiaceae), are aquatic plants, some floating. **Branched Bur-reed** *Sparganium erectum* (11) grows by fresh water. Stiff-stemmed, its tiny stemless flowers on leafy spikes swell into bur-like fruits. **Unbranched Bur-reed** *S. emersum* (12) has leaves that float on the water.

Common Horsetail *Equisetum arvense* (13) (Horsetail Family, Equisetaceae) likes dry places. Fertile stems are brown, unbranched, barren ones green. **Giant Horsetail** *E. telmateia* (15), larger, paler and more robust, prefers damp places.

False Bulrush *Typha latifolia* (14) (Reedmace Family, Typhaceae), a swamp and small-pond plant with long, stiff greyish leaves overtopping brown spike of female flowers and fluffy green male ones. **Lesser Bulrush** *T. angustifolia* (16) likes a similar habitat but has narrower, paler leaves and a slimmer spike.

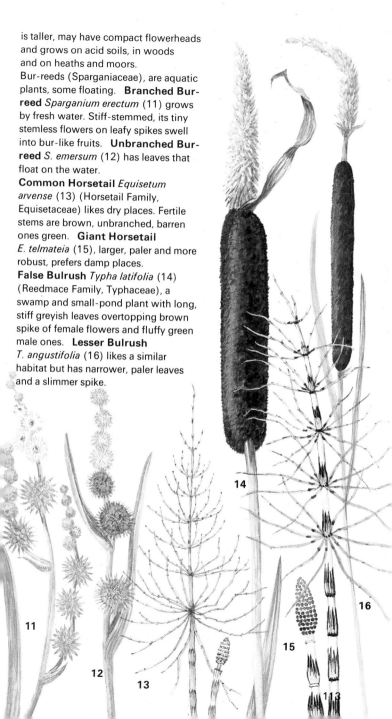

11

12

13

14

15

16

SEDGES & COTTON-GRASSES

The Sedge Family (Cyperaceae) are unbranched perennials, most with narrow grass-like leaves, but some, more rush-like, with the leaves reduced to sheaths. The tiny flowers grouped in spikes or heads, are conspicuous only when their yellow anthers appear in spring. Unlike grasses, sedges have stems often three-sided, never hollow and lacking leaf-joints.

Common Club-Rush or Bulrush *Scirpus lacustris* (1) grows in rivers and lakes and was formerly used in basket-making. **Sea Club-Rush** *S. maritimus* (4) has leaves and grows by the sea. The fluffy white fruiting heads of the **Common Cotton-grass** *Eriophorum angustifolium* (3) and

Harestail Cotton-grass
E. vaginatum (2) warn of the danger of
the bogs where they grow.
Greater and **Lesser Pond Sedges**
Carex riparia (5) and *C. acutiformis* (6)
have greyish leaves and grow by rivers
and lakes and in marshes. **Cyperus
Sedge** or Hop Sedge *C. pseudo-
cyperus* (16) is more local in similar
places.
Bottle Sedge *C. rostrata* (15) is
frequent round lake shores in the north,
but **Bladder Sedge** *C. vesicaria* (8)
grows more in peaty places. **Greater
Tussock Sedge** *C. paniculata* (12)
makes substantial tussocks, 60–120 cm
high, in wet places. **False Fox Sedge**
C. otrubae (13) is common in damp
grassy places; the true Fox Sedge
C. vulpina is rare. Graceful **Pendulous
Sedge** *C. pendula* (14) grows in damp
woodland rides. **Wood Sedge**
C. sylvatica (7) is widespread and
common in woods. **Glaucous Sedge**
C. flacca (9) and **Carnation Sedge**
C. panicea (10) both have greyish
leaves and grow in dry chalk and
limestone grassland and marshy places
respectively. **Sand Sedge**
C. arenaria (11) is common on dunes,
especially by the sea.

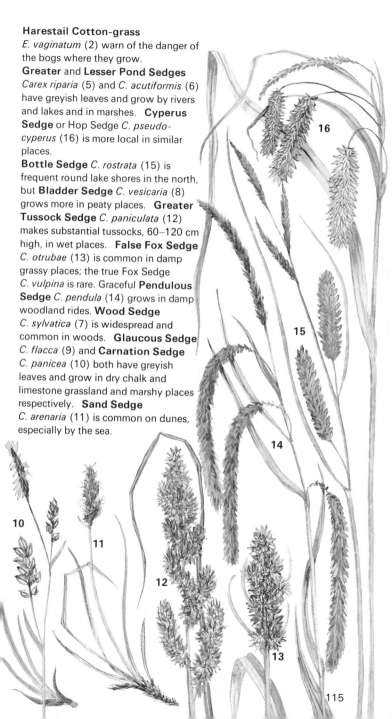

GRASSES

Members of the Grass Family (Gramineae) usually have hollow stems, swollen at the junctions of the long narrow parallel-veined leaves. Their tiny flowers are petalless, and arranged in opposite rows in spikelets, sometimes clumped into heads. Their yellow stamens are the only colourful parts. Most grasses grow in a close sward, usually of several species mixed.

The **Common Reed** *Phragmites australis* (1) is our largest grass, and makes extensive reed-beds in wet places. Its dried stems are used for thatching. **Reed Canary-grass** *Phalaris arundinacea* (8) and **Reed Sweet-grass** *Glyceria maxima* (4) are two other tall waterside grasses. **Purple Moor-grass** *Molinia caerulea* (2) is characteristic of bogs and wet heaths and moors.

Marram *Ammophila arenaria* (3) is common on coastal sand dunes and plays an important part in binding the sand and preventing blow-outs.

Cocksfoot *Dactylis glomerata* (5) is one of the commonest wayside grasses, also important as a fodder plant. **False Oat-grass** *Arrhenatherum elatius* (6) is equally common in rough grassy places, but less valuable for grazing. **Giant Fescue** *Festuca gigantea* (7) and **Hairy Brome** *Bromus ramosus* (9) are both tall grasses of shady places. Hairy Brome is the more graceful, and easily told by its hairy leaf-sheaths. **Upright Brome** *B. erectus* (10) is the characteristic tall grass of chalk and limestone grassland, sometimes dominating extensive areas.

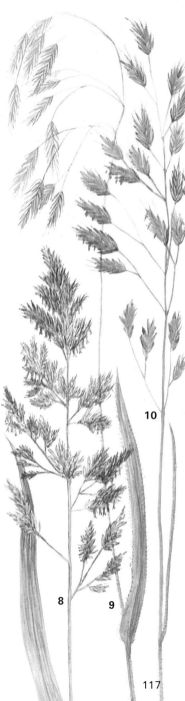

10

8   9

118

GRASSES

Floating Sweet-grass *Glyceria fluitans* (1) is a common grass of ponds and other still water; its leaves often float on the surface.

Red Fescue *Festuca rubra* (2) and **Sheep's Fescue** *F. ovina* (4) are two of the commonest grasses of heaths, moors and downs, red fescue being also an important element in lowland meadows and pastures.

Smooth Meadow-grass *Poa pratensis* (5) and **Rough Meadow-grass** *P. trivialis* (6) are another pair of common grasses, smooth meadow-grass growing in more open and rough meadow-grass in shadier places, and neither of them actually in meadows.

False Brome *Brachypodium sylvaticum* (9) is highly characteristic of woods and shady places, where it is very common.

Barren Brome *Bromus sterilis* (3) and **Soft Brome** *B. hordeaceus* (7) are both common grasses of waste places, Soft Brome also sometimes appearing in swards with other species. **Common Couch** or Twitch *Agropyron repens* (8) is one of the gardener's worst weeds; its far-creeping roots strongly resist his fork.

Timothy *Phleum pratense* (10) and **Meadow Foxtail** *Alopecurus pratensis* (12) are two common grassland species. Timothy flowers in July, when its pollen is the cause of great discomfort to hay-fever sufferers, and Meadow Foxtail in April, when it is one of the first grasses to put forth its yellow stamens, which later turn orange.

Creeping Bent *Agrostis stolonifera* (11) and **Common Bent** *A. tenuis* (13) are two more common grasses widely found in meadows and pastures. Creeping Bent also grows in damp places, and Common Bent on heaths and moors.

119

GRASSES

Perennial Rye-Grass *Lolium perenne.* (1) is one of the most important fodder grasses for the grazier, and also grows widely on roadsides and in waste places. **Crested Dogstail** *Cynosurus cristatus* (4) and **Sweet Vernal Grass** *Anthoxanthum odoratum* (9) are two more important constituents of the sward of many meadows and pastures.

Annual Meadow-Grass *Poa annua* (2) is annual (most grasses are perennials) and is a very common weed of bare places, flowering all through the season and in mild winters. **Wall Barley** *Hordeum murinum* (7) is also a common wayside plant where there is some lime in the soil, often growing at the foot of walls.

Wood Meadow-Grass *Poa nemoralis* (3) and **Wood Melick** *Melica uniflora* (6) are both frequent in woods and shady places, especially on limy soils.

Quaking Grass or Totter Grass *Briza media* (5), named from the constant movement of its spikelets on their wiry stalks even in the slightest breeze, is characteristic of chalk and limestone grassland. **Mat Grass** *Nardus stricta* (11), on the other hand, grows exclusively in highly acid soils on moors and heaths. **Yorkshire Fog** *Holcus lanatus* (8) is so called from the effect of its pale purple flowerheads growing in a mass on the rather bare open ground it prefers. Its relative **Creeping Soft-Grass** *H. mollis* (10) grows only in shady places on rather acid soils.

10

11

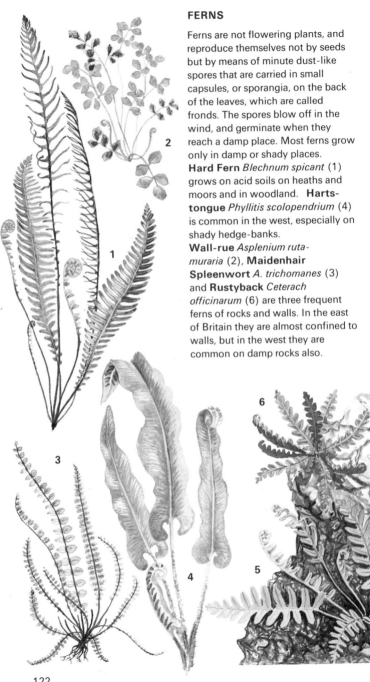

FERNS

Ferns are not flowering plants, and reproduce themselves not by seeds but by means of minute dust-like spores that are carried in small capsules, or sporangia, on the back of the leaves, which are called fronds. The spores blow off in the wind, and germinate when they reach a damp place. Most ferns grow only in damp or shady places.

Hard Fern *Blechnum spicant* (1) grows on acid soils on heaths and moors and in woodland. **Harts-tongue** *Phyllitis scolopendrium* (4) is common in the west, especially on shady hedge-banks.

Wall-rue *Asplenium ruta-muraria* (2), **Maidenhair Spleenwort** *A. trichomanes* (3) and **Rustyback** *Ceterach officinarum* (6) are three frequent ferns of rocks and walls. In the east of Britain they are almost confined to walls, but in the west they are common on damp rocks also.

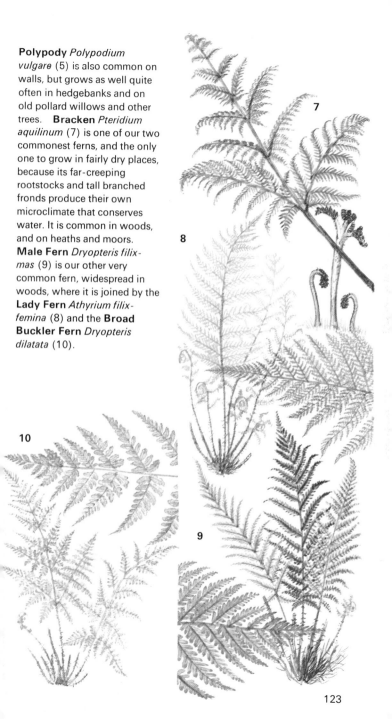

Polypody *Polypodium vulgare* (5) is also common on walls, but grows as well quite often in hedgebanks and on old pollard willows and other trees.   **Bracken** *Pteridium aquilinum* (7) is one of our two commonest ferns, and the only one to grow in fairly dry places, because its far-creeping rootstocks and tall branched fronds produce their own microclimate that conserves water. It is common in woods, and on heaths and moors. **Male Fern** *Dryopteris filix-mas* (9) is our other very common fern, widespread in woods, where it is joined by the **Lady Fern** *Athyrium filix-femina* (8) and the **Broad Buckler Fern** *Dryopteris dilatata* (10).

123

Index of English Names

125